— THE —
MARRIAGE MANUAL

TONY BOER LCSW PIP

— THE —
MARRIAGE MANUAL

HOW TO GET THE MOST OUT OF YOUR MARRIAGE:
A TROUBLE SHOOTING GUIDE WHEN PROBLEMS ARISE

Copyright © 2021 by Tony Boer LCSW PIP

ISBN Softcover: 978-1-7344127-7-2
Ebook ISBN: 978-1-7344127-9-6

All rights reserved. No part of this book may be reproduced or transmitted in any form or by any means, electronic or mechanical, including photocopying, recording or by any information storage and retrieval system, without permission in writing from the copyright owner. For information on distribution rights, royalties, derivative works or licensing opportunities on behalf of this content or work, please contact the publisher at the address below.

Printed in the United States of America.

Cover and Layout Design: Story Seven
Editor: Kaylyn Mehlhaff

Although the author and publisher have made every effort to ensure that the information and advice in this book was correct and accurate at press time, the author and publisher do not assume and hereby disclaim any liability to any party for any loss, damage, or disruption caused from acting upon the information in this book or by errors or omissions, whether such errors or omissions result from negligence, accident, or any other cause.

2000 S. Sycamore Suite 101
Sioux Falls, SD 57110

Dedication

This book is dedicated to my loving wife—thanks for always being by my side, cheering me on, and being patient with my mistakes. You have shown and taught me incredible things about what a great marriage looks like.

TABLE OF CONTENTS

Introduction XI

PART I – GETTING STARTED – TOOLS YOU WILL NEED

Tool #1: You 04
Tool #2: Communication 24
Tool #3: Know How to Fight 56
Tool #4: Grace 78
Tool #5: Commitment .86
Optional Equipment 96

PART 2 – TROUBLESHOOTING GUIDE

Time 104
Children 108
No Help 112
In-Laws/Parents 116
Money 120
Big Life Changes 132
Sex 138
Affairs 150
Addictions 164
Abuse 168
Religious Differences 172
Mental Health Issues 180
Married Later in life 186

Step-Children. 192

PART 3 – ROUTINE MAINTENANCE

PART 4 – WARRANTY INFORMATION

Conclusion 224

Appendices 226

About the Author 244

— INTRODUCTION —

THE GOAL OF THIS BOOK.

Hey, thanks for picking up *The Marriage Manual!* I'm assuming that since you are reading this, you have an interest in marriages—probably your own—and you want to know how they work. Well, then this book is for you. *The Marriage Manual* is written like the instruction manual you get when you buy something new. Please don't do with this book what many do with most instruction manuals: toss it aside and start messing around with the new phone, dishwasher, or computer you just purchased—pushing buttons and trying things out.

Let's say you just got a brand new television. What do you do with that shiny new flatscreen? Most people plug it in and start watching TV. Some in this scenario will say to themselves, I know how this works, they'll plug the TV in, and away they'll go. Others simply figure it out as they go along. Do you throw the manual away? Typically you end up telling yourself something like, this thing has a five-year warranty, all the information is in there, so we should probably keep it for a little while, so you throw it in a drawer and forget about it. Then something terrible happens, your TV has a strange logo on the screen that keeps flashing, but you don't know what it means. What do you do? You go find the manual and look up what your TV is trying to tell you!

Or what about this scenario: You want to watch something on your phone, and your kid comes into the room and tells you, "You know you can watch that on your TV, right?"

Your super-techy child then shows you how to cast the show you're watching on your phone onto your TV and pretty soon you're watching your phone on the big screen!

"I never knew my TV could do that!" you exclaim. "I wonder what else this thing can do?!"

You then go find the manual to look up all the features your TV can do. How long did you go without knowing everything your TV was capable of? What have you been missing out on?

Here's the thing: your marriage has so many more features and cool tricks than your TV!

That is the goal of this book: it's a manual for your marriage. **Don't treat your marriage like a TV.** But most people do exactly that. They get married and think, I know what this is, and they start going through married life thinking they will just figure it out as they go. The person who views marriage this way only really thinks about their marriage when things are going poorly. Unfortunately, this means they are not getting everything out of their marriage that they could.

 **DON'T TREAT YOUR MARRIAGE LIKE A TV.**

The goal of this book.

What special features of your marriage are you missing out on? Do you even know? Have you just been doing routine maintenance on your marriage? Did you install your marriage correctly? If you are only now looking at the manual, that probably means you're getting signs that it's not working correctly, hence the manual.

Icon	Description
⚠	**WARNING**
❗	**PRECAUTION**
📝	**TAKE NOTES**
📖	**REFER BACK TO INSTRUCTION MANUAL**

Well, you're in luck! This is the manual! However, there is one problem. This is not a repair manual! That is something entirely different.

When you go television shopping, the people working will tell you, "Yes, we have TVs. We have this refurbished one that was broken, we fixed it, and it's working now, but it doesn't come with a warranty. It is, however, a little cheaper, but we can't guarantee how long it will last."

Or you can go shopping for a TV and buy a brand new one that comes with a guarantee that it will last a long time if your take care of it. Which TV do you pick?!

It's the same with your marriage. I don't want you to simply fix your old marriage that isn't working so well. I want you to create a brand new one. **You wouldn't buy a refurbished TV, don't settle for a refurbished marriage.**

My hope is that when you are done with this book, if you follow the instructions you will have a healthy, functioning marriage. This is a new marriage for you. This is a new model with new features. It is not going to be like your old one. That is an important point to remember. People will often say, "I liked the old (computer, TV, oven, marriage, etc.) better. It didn't always work well, but I was comfortable with it, and it was predictable." As you develop a new marriage, you will need a new mindset

NEW MINDSET.

Getting into this new mindset is probably the biggest obstacle I see in couples coming to marriage counseling. They have a hard time letting go. Just like when you are buying a

The goal of this book.

TV, you tell the salesperson, "Well, my old one did this, will this one do that?"

When couples come into marriage therapy, I will often tell them that I am not here to fix their old marriage because clearly, that one is not working, which is why they are usually in my office. Instead I propose that I would love to help them create a new marriage. This usually sounds good to the couple right away, but is often derailed with comments later on, such as, "He always does this," or, "I know what she is going to say, so why bother?"

 BUILD THE MARRIAGE, NOT FIX YOUR SPOUSE.

These assumptions may have been true in the past, but not in this new marriage. Breaking old habits is hard and will often sabotage your ability to have something new. When couples are building a new marriage, they need to make sure they are willing to embark on the journey. It always helps to focus not on how your spouse acts, but on how you are acting. I want you to think only about yourself and your actions when talking about how your old marriage used to do this or that. Focus on yourself. This is a manual to build a healthy marriage, not a manual to complain about or try and fix your spouse! **Build the marriage, not fix your spouse.** If you can keep this concept in your head, it will help you from falling into the trap of trying to simply refurbish your spouse to get a few more years out of him or her.

You don't want to do things differently for a while, only to fall back into your old way of doing marriage and return to therapy a couple years later with the same problems. If you want to have a new marriage and would like a guide to help you get there, then read on. I would like to help you have a healthy, functioning marriage, and this is the manual to do just that.

The Marriage Manual is written exactly like that instruction manual you get with your new TV. Don't cast it aside until you are stuck and have to refer to it. Take some time to read and learn about how a healthy marriage is set up and installed. Along the way you'll find the tools that you need. The things you need to do for routine maintenance. How to troubleshoot potential problems. And finally, how to make your marriage last a long time.

The goal of this book.

— NOTES —

—PART 1—
GETTING STARTED

Before you get started, you will need to make sure you have the right tools for assembling your marriage. To correctly install a healthy marriage, you will need some tools. If you don't have them, you can go get them now. You cannot assemble a healthy marriage without the right tools. Any task goes better when you have the right tools. Don't underestimate how important each tool is to completing the job. If you don't use the right tools, you might not fully put something together, it may break too soon, only work partially, or even not work at all. This is true for appliances and for marriages.

— NOTES —

— TOOL #1 —

YOU!

The very first tool you need in a healthy marriage is YOU! You cannot assemble a healthy marriage if you do not first have someone who wants a healthy marriage. Do not underestimate the power of YOU and *your* perspective in impacting relationships. I previously wrote a book for therapists teaching them how to learn about themselves so that they can connect with clients to help them better[1]. It is no different in a marriage. I assume that since you're reading this book, you want a healthy marriage. But are you ready for one? Remember, we are not looking at your spouse to see if he is prepared. Are you prepared? Do you genuinely want a new, healthy marriage? If the answer is yes, then you need to spend some time identifying who you are. What is your previous history with relationships? What did you learn from your family? Often when I do premarital counseling, we spend some time talking about your family growing up. There are some essential elements that you need to identify and know about yourself first

---

[1] Boer, Tony. The Art of Therapy: A Practical How-To Guide for Therapists. Story Seven Publishing, 2020.

if you are going to be in the best possible emotional shape for a healthy relationship.

A question to help you understand yourself more is, what type of family did you come from? Do you come from a "broken" family? "Broken" is a potent term that the world uses to describe a family that doesn't have both a mom and a dad.

Why do we call these types of marriages broken? What is broken? I think broken is the term the world has chosen to use to try to convey that if you come from this type of marriage, you are missing something. I don't think this kind of family is necessarily "broken," but "missing something" is a better way of putting it.

What are you missing? You are missing out on seeing your birthparents loving each other and modeling what marriage looks like. Often your parents' relationship is your first exposure to what marriage is. Even if you have two parents living together and married, it doesn't mean their marriage is healthy. What did the marital relationship that you observed growing up teach you? Did your parents show respect to each other? How did they do that? The first big, central question you need to ask yourself is: what did I learn from them?

Another way to ask the question is, would you like the same marriage as your parents? Most people say no. So if your biggest role models and teachers are your parents and you don't want a relationship like theirs, what are you going to do? Spend some time thinking about how your parents interacted with each other. What did you like? What did you not like? If I ask you, what are your dad's views of how a marriage should run? What are your mom's? What kind of answers would your give?

I will often give couples a little script of questions to identify what their life was like growing up and how those experiences impacted their views about marriage. All the ways your parents influenced you might be surprising as you slow down and start to see them showing up all over your actions and thoughts.

The following is an example of how your family of origin can impact your marriage. Awareness of what you learned about marriage growing up affects how you interact with your spouse.

DAVE AND MADDIE.

Here is a typical conversation between the two:

Maddie: I think we should go out with Sue and Tom this weekend, what do you think?

Dave: If that's what you want to do, that's fine.

Maddie: Well, what do you want to do? Do you have a better idea?

Dave: I said that's fine. Whatever you like is good with me!

Maddie: Well, we don't have to go out with them! We can do something else!

Dave: No, that's fine

Maddie: Don't you have any input on what we do?

Dave: (sensing that Maddie is getting angry and trying to calm things down) I don't care what we do. Whatever you want is fine.

Maddie: (increasingly frustrated that she is not getting any real input from Dave) Can you just tell me what you would like to do this weekend? Why is that so difficult? You can never just tell me what you want to do. I have to be in charge and make all the decisions. If you cared at all, you would put some effort in and help me out once in and while!

Dave: Help you?! I'm always helping you and doing things for you. You never notice or appreciate all the sacrifices that I make for you.

Now the fight is on! Here is a little of the backstory behind Dave and Maddie's argument and how their past and family history impacts their current relationship:

Dave and Maddie have been married for six years. Dave grew up in an alcoholic family. He was taught to keep the peace and never get any unwanted attention. When Dave did get unwanted attention, his father would yell at and belittle him. His mother was codependent and willing to try to make things as normal as possible for her kids, so Dave's dad had as little contact with the family while he was drunk as possible. Dave was taught not only to keep the peace, but also not to cause trouble. He was instructed not to share his feelings, as those emotions were unpredictable and usually caused fights.

How does this behavior work now in his marriage? In some ways, it works well. Dave is always checking in with his wife, making sure that she is doing okay. He has taken on the role of his mom, trying to make sure things always go as smoothly as possible for his wife. The downside is that Dave rarely shares his feelings. He is fearful that he may say something that Maddie does not like. When asked what he is thinking or feeling, he will frequently defer to Maddie to take the temperature of the room and simply follow her lead with feelings.

Maddie grew up in a pretty typical family, but she often felt insecure. She felt like she was not popular and did not quite fit in with the cool kids. Maddie's parents would constantly give her ideas about how to be more outgoing or tell her different ways she could act. Their advice on trying to do things differently added to her insecurity. Maddie grew up feeling picked on and helpless. She decided that no one was going to tell her how to act—she was not going to be dependent on anyone. Maddie went from feeling powerless growing up to making sure she was in control as an adult. This has impacted her marriage to Dave in a variety of ways. She was not going to be dependent on anyone again.

In this scenario and others like it, Dave was frustrated because Maddie never acted like she needed anything from him. Maddie was frustrated because Dave never shared his feelings with her. They kept acting as though they were still in their family of origin. This cycle kept repeating itself, and neither one was aware of how their past contributed to the problem. Dave understanding that he can share feelings and nothing terrible will happen will make Maddie feel more connected. When she is more connected, she is more willing to spend time with him. Maddie learning that she needs to express some feelings and ask for help with life from her husband will cause him to share more feelings. Often couples can see how the dysfunctional pattern affects their marriage, but they have trouble seeing that this pattern can work in the opposite direction just as quickly.

Learning about how your family of origin frames how you think and impacts your current perspective on marriage can begin to help you see how you bring that to your current marriage—not only identifying, but also changing the dysfunctional patterns you may have learned. You have to be willing to "go there." Don't be afraid to take a good look at yourself.

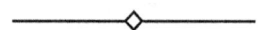

Once you have identified what you can learn from your family of origin, you need to take inventory and see where you are at. What is your attitude towards marriage? Are you in it forever? Do you simply hope to get a few good years out of it? Have you always dreamed of being married, or is it something that just kind of happened? Your attitude towards these questions will shed a lot of light on how healthy your marriage will be. What is your definition of a happy, healthy marriage? I keep saying that we are going to build a healthy marriage, but what does that mean to you?

After your attitude on marriage is solidified, you need to think about your beliefs or goals in terms of what you hope or want your marriage to look like. I will often ask couples in premarital therapy what their marriage goals are. Often they don't have any goals! Crazy! Think about this, you have goals for every other area of your life. Why not your marriage? It's no wonder people get discouraged and frustrated in marriage—they don't have anything to shoot for! They are just hoping their marriage is good, not even sure what "good" means.

If you are a 20 years-old just starting out in life and I ask you what your career goals are, I will hear things like, "I hope to work as a nurse for a while, get some experience, and then get my master's degree and maybe eventually become a nurse practitioner to work with a doctor in a clinic." Or, "I want to work on cars, so I'm working a lot of bad hours for a dealership, but I hope to earn enough money to open my own garage someday."

If I ask a couple what their family goals are, they will say things like, "We want to be married for a few years and then have two kids two years apart, first a boy then a girl." (Remember, these are young people in love, you and I know having two kids two years apart that are a boy and a girl is not realistic, but at least it's a goal!) The couple will have financial goals such as paying off student loans, then buying a house, and hopefully saving money for their kids to go to college or to take some vacations, finishing up with having enough to retire on. Again, really great, specific goals. Frequently couples will have talked about these goals together and they may have even started working on them together. Then I ask about their marriage goals, and I get blank stares. Marriage is the only thing that people tend to make backward goals for. What I mean is most people have the goal of starting on top and going down from there. Couples say things like, "We want to make the honeymoon last as long as possible, raise some kids, and hopefully still love each other when we retire!" Do you see how that goal goes on a downward spiral and all the other goals go on an upward spiral?

When working on the tool of you, you need to have some clear goals of what you want your healthy marriage to look like. These goals need to be yours, ones that you want or need in your marriage. Not everyone's goals need to be the same, just like everyone's career goals are not the same. Some people want to have significant careers and money, while others wish to have small careers and tons of family time—there is no right or wrong answer, but you need to have some goals when it comes to your marriage.

Some marital goals I would suggest you take a look at could be:

- Become so good at communication that you can talk to your spouse about ANYTHING and EVERYTHING, including your hurts, insecurities, fears, sexual desires, dreams, prayers, and annoying things that your spouse does.
- Be on the same page with raising children. What types of qualities and characteristics do you want your children to learn?
- Be able to tell your spouse what you can and can't do for them.
- Grow to where you can understand and know what your spouse can and can't give you.

These are just a few of the goals you can come up with! Starting to have some goals gives you a place to start working on things now—it's just a matter of taking those big goals and making them into smaller goals and completing the steps.

Now that you have these goals, you need to ask yourself if you're ready to go after them. That may sound like an easy answer. Yes!! But not so fast, slow down. To start working towards your goals means you have to change what you've been doing. Are you willing to change? I did not ask if your spouse needs to change. Remember, this first tool is YOU! Are you ready to do things radically different, not merely a redo of the same old stuff? **Remember, no refurbishing, you are worth more than that.** Take some time to think this through,

REMEMBER, NO REFURBISHING

it's super important. We are calibrating your healthy marriage, and it starts with this new reframing that you are willing to do things differently. Go slow. Say it out loud if you have to:

> I, (___name___) am willing to do things radically different in my marriage. I will work on goals. I will work on identifying my role in what I need to do to have a healthy relationship. I am willing to get hurt to accomplish this.

What? Hurt?! Yep! Are you willing to go that far? Are you ready to get your heart stomped on to have a good marriage? Some of you have had your heart stomped on multiple times already. Are you willing to do it again? If you decide not to read on after this point, you have settled for a refurbished marriage. You can do that without this manual. To change means to be willing to do things so different that you are engaged and participating in the relationship regardless of if your spouse is or not. There have been many couples I have seen in therapy that want the marriage to be different. Still, their marriage fails because they are waiting for their spouse to change or show signs of doing things differently before they are willing to "jump back in" to their marriage. **There is no safe way to be in a relationship.**

 **THERE IS NO SAFE WAY TO BE IN A RELATIONSHIP.**

I will periodically give you examples of couples and the situations they have been dealing with to illustrate my points. Just like in other manuals, these examples will sometimes give you a picture of what a marriage should look like, while others will show you what not to do. Please know that I have changed the names, details, and identifying information in every example. If you think you know the person I am writing about, you don't—the exact scenario you are reading about does not exist in real life. If you recognize yourself in the examples, then I'm glad—you are starting to change!

This next story is an example of not only how past relationships can impact your future ones, but also how those past relationships can cause you to sabotage a healthy one. Past relationships can be with family, previous partners, or even past friendships. What you learned from that person or people can be reused in your next relationship, good or bad. But learned dysfunction can go on to cause dysfunction in future relationships.

JACK AND JILL.

Jack and Jill have been married for 10 years. Jack has a great job working in a water treatment plant and Jill stays home with their two boys, who are one and four years-old. Jill grew up in a dysfunctional home that didn't have a lot of rules or expectations. Her mother was passive-aggressive towards her. She would frequently say things that would let Jill know she was not happy with her, showing Jill that she was not doing what her mother expected. Her mother would make Jill feel like she was not good enough.

Jack grew up in a structured house where everyone in the family was expected to be successful. He had to perform and solve any problems that were getting in his way. Jack and Jill came into counseling because Jill was caught sending inappropriate pictures to two guys. There had not been any physical contact between Jill or the two guys. Both of the people she had been sending pictures to were old acquaintances that did not live near her. After I spent some time with them, Jack shared his frustrations about Jill frequently lying. He was angry because he felt like the lies were always over small things. Things like what Jill did during the day, what she spent money on, etc. Jill was frustrated because she felt like she could never please or make Jack happy with anything she did.

Here is an example of a typical conversation between Jack and Jill:

Jack: What did you do today?

Jill: Not much, just ran some errands.

Jack: Where did you go?

Jill: Just got groceries, gas, and returned some things to Target!

Jack: Did you get anything at Target?

Jill: Oh, just a few things that we were running low on.

Jack: That's good. How much did you spend?

Jill: Well, I don't really know because I had some returns and got some credit back.

Jack: *(getting frustrated because he does not feel like he is getting a good answer and is starting to sense that she may have spent a lot)* You don't know how much money you spent at Target? That can't be true!

Jill: *(feeling defensive and fearful that she has disappointed Jack and trying to avoid this)* I didn't keep exact track since I returned stuff and bought things we needed. I didn't get anything that we didn't need. You always think that I'm wasting money. I never once ask you how much you spend on things. You always make it so I can't please you. I'll go and get the receipt.

The crazy thing about this argument is that when he looked at the receipt, Jack was totally fine with the purchases, and there was not a problem with the amount. Unfortunately, the argument had already done its damage.

When you look at their pasts, you can see that Jill learned to deal with her mother by telling her lies and avoiding her mother's comments and judgments. Her mom made comments but never held Jill accountable or followed up with anything, so avoiding and lying worked with her mother. This was also how Jill handled previous relationships. Whenever things became difficult, she would avoid the situation. Sometimes her boyfriends would forget, or sometimes they would break up with her, so she never really had to change. This behavior usually worked just like it did with her mother—making things less tense at home. But these tactics did not work with Jack. He would follow through on things and hold his wife accountable for what she said. Jack is used to being held responsible and solving problems. He does not understand how it can feel judgmental to Jill when he is attacking a problem and trying to fix it. When the problem he is attacking involves his wife, Jack sends the message that she is the problem. Jack needs to learn how to communicate differently with his wife. Jill needs to understand what healthy accountability is like in a relationship.

Jill has to understand that when you are trying to be in a functional relationship, you can't use learned dysfunctional tactics—they will not work. She was never in trouble with Jack in the receipt scenario. But her history taught her that she might be, so she panicked and handled Jack the same way she had handled her mom and past boyfriends.

Functional requires functional. Dysfunction works well with dysfunction. You cannot mix and match— the two do not cross over. What happens if you are trying to loosen a bolt with the wrong size wrench? If you have a metric wrench but you're trying to remove an English-sized bolt, what happens? You may reduce it or even get it removed, but you will strip the bolt, and it won't work in the future. You stripped the bolt because the tool you were using was not the right one. If you are trying to have a healthy, functional relationship you need to use healthy, functional tools. You need to know yourself. What things are you still using that may have worked when you were younger but are not good things to carry into a current relationship? Jill needed to learn this concept.

Now, it is important to remember that you can switch back to past behaviors if you need to, depending on who you are with.

Jill needs to have functional interactions with her husband but not necessarily with her mom. When she visits her mom, it may be best not to respond to her mother's passive-aggressiveness at all. However, when she is home with her husband, Jill will need to respond to his feelings.

Remember the above example and how it relates to knowing yourself and what you learned growing up or in previous relationships. How can those lessons be repeated? If you know yourself better, that tool will help you when you are in a relationship with another person.

Marriage would be easy if there was just one of you, but marriage is not one of you—there are two needed in a healthy marriage. Hopefully by now you have learned who you are and why you are the way you are. Now you need to take all that knowledge and apply it to your spouse. What is your spouse's personality? What is he like? How did he become the way he is? How did his family and upbringing impact him? Think about questions you asked yourself to learn about yourself and why you are the way you are. You should know the answers to those same questions regarding your spouse. Is he a morning person? Extrovert? Conservative? Emotional? Patient? Hyperactive? Etc.

Now, remember you won't always like the answers to these questions about your spouse. Opposites attract. One of the biggest keys to having a healthy marriage is understanding this concept. You tend to be attracted to someone who is totally different from you. This means that although you may be able to list all the characteristics or qualities of your spouse, you will probably not understand or like all of them!

We have all heard that opposites attract, but I think it would be helpful if we spent a little time looking at this concept more in-depth to understand why this is and what role it plays in a marriage. Opposites attract typically works like this: You are a person who is always a little bit worried about things and how they will turn out. You tend to need to be in control of situations because you like to be organized as much as possible. You worry that things might not go smoothly. You think it would be helpful to have someone in a relationship who's similar, who also likes to know the plan and is worried about things going smoothly. You think you will be attracted to someone like that, right? Wrong! Instead you will be attracted to the person who is relaxed, does not worry, and typically does not have an identified or specific plan. You will see him as calm and peaceful. You want more of that in your life, so you bring that into your life in the form of a relationship with a person like this.

Sounds great, right? You now have someone in your life who will help you relax, enjoy life, and bring some peace to it. That is true, but anyone who has been in a relationship long enough knows that the very things that attract you to someone are also the things that drive you crazy about them. Often, we try to turn the person we married into someone who acts and thinks more like us. The person who is relaxed, calm, and peaceful is now being called unorganized, not caring, and lazy. **The critical lesson here is remembering that it is not a good idea to try to make your spouse more like** you. **The more you change your spouse, the less attracted to them you will actually be!**

I will often tell couples in counseling that I don't want to change them too much because that could cause big problems. Think about this, **do you really want to be married to yourself?!** What would that look like if the two of you acted and thought the same? Often when we are frustrated and not in the right spot with our spouse, we will dream of what that level of similarity would be like. Unfortunately, we don't spend enough time really thinking through that dream. Yes, it would be great to have a spouse who is responsible and ready on time. That would be so nice and peaceful. But take that dream just a little further and you'll realize that would also mean that you now have to do things that your spouse had typically been doing. Your spouse is currently the relaxed one who keeps things fun and makes everyone feel at ease. But if you suddenly become the relaxed one too, someone will now have to do the organizational tasks that kept you up late, or do you both just forget about those and not do them? Hopefully they were not too important because typically the other person was not even aware what of those tasks were in the first place!

You can't have two leaders and no followers. You can't have two talkers and no listeners. You can't have two laid-back optimists who don't stay on track. And you can't have two realists who never relax. The goal is to begin to see your spouse as someone who is different than you, but not worse or better. Just different.

DO YOU REALLY WANT TO BE MARRIED TO YOURSELF?!

This understanding of who you are and who your spouse is will become vital as we continue this manual and work to build a healthy marriage. It is critical to have a perspective where you understand that your spouse is not doing things simply to make you mad or annoy you. I have seen countless couples who are convinced that their spouse is only doing things a certain way because they know it bugs them. Think about that for a minute. We all have that feeling sometimes, but you cannot let it grow. Do you really think the person that loves and cares about you the most is purposely doing things to annoy you? Why is your spouse annoying you? It is not because they are bored and there is nothing to watch on TV. No! They are acting that way because that is who they are. Beginning to see your spouse as someone who is different than you and not trying to change them, but instead trying to figure out what they are thinking will save you from arguments in the future. Have the approach of figuring out where your spouse's behavior is coming from and how that can help you. It is a perspective you probably never would have come up with on your own. Remember also that your spouse is not thinking from your perspective, so you will have to be willing to share your thoughts and feelings with them. Knowing the right way to share is our next tool.

The Marriage Manual

The more you can learn to use this first tool—understanding you, who you are, and why you are the way you are—and, in turn, knowing that you have a spouse who is not you and approaches the world in a different and unique way, can broaden your understanding of marriage and make your life richer and fuller. You are now on your way to building the foundation of a healthy marriage.

YOU!

— NOTES —

— NOTES —

— TOOL #2 —

COMMUNICATION

The second tool you will need in order to have a healthy marriage is the ability to communicate. You are going to need to be able to share with your significant other not only who you are and why you act the way you do, but you will also need to be able to communicate how you are feeling. This is especially challenging because your feelings will change—they will not always be predictable, and at times you will not even be able to explain why you feel the way you feel. You will also be explaining your feelings to someone who typically sees the world differently than you do. This is why you will often hear people say they need to work on communication or that they have communication issues in their marriage. What do they mean by this? Ed Wheat, in his book The First Years of Forever wrote, "researchers believe that 90% of all marriage counseling involves the attempt to restore communication or teach couples to communicate effectively for the first time." [2]

---

[2] Wheat, Ed. The First Years of Forever. Grand Rapids, Michigan, Zondervan, 1988

Knowing that communication is essential to marriage can only get you so far if you do not know how to use this tool correctly. **Communication is a tool in the marriage that can be mishandled easily.** If you use this tool wrong, just like any other tool, you can do more damage than you intend. To use this tool of communication correctly, you will first need to know how to use it and then practice using the tool so you become more comfortable.

There are some fundamental communication skills that you will need to learn before moving on to the more complex skills. You will find these necessary skills in a variety of books and articles. They are in lists, bullet points, handy acronyms, etc. I will go over each of these stills using a basic format, and if you need additional communication skills to add to your toolkit, I've included a few resources in the back of the book.

- **Complete attention:** Half is not enough. Half listening means half hearing what the other person is trying to relay to you. If you are not paying attention to what your spouse is saying, it will lead to misunderstanding and the wrong interpretation of what your spouse is trying to say. If your spouse is taking the time to talk, make sure you are sending the message that you are willing to hear them and take the time to give the topic they are talking about the attention that it deserves.

- **Eye Contact:** Similar to complete attention, eye contact deserves a spot all by itself. You can communicate a lot by merely giving your spouse the respect their words deserve by looking them in the eye.

 ## YOU CAN INTERRUPT SOMEONE WITH BODY LANGUAGE

- **No interruptions:** Interruptions when your spouse is talking to you will lead to frustration, plus when you interrupt, you're usually jumping to conclusions that are frequently wrong. Often interruptions will occur when you believe you know what the other person is going to say and are already forming a response or comeback to what they're saying. Remember, you should be trying to figure out what your spouse is sharing and why in this situation right now. What just happened? When your spouse is communicating their feelings, rarely should you interrupt—don't you want to hear what they're feeling? In counseling, I will at times have a wife who would like to connect more with her husband, and she's frustrated that he's not talking about or sharing his feelings. He will begin to share his feelings in the counseling session, but she will interrupt when he begins to share and start to talk over him. The husband then shuts down. Sometimes this happens so fast you'll almost miss it. An interruption can sometimes be as simple as a deep breath or looking away from your spouse. **You can interrupt someone with body language.** In fact, body language can be more disruptive than actual words.

- **Repeat what you have heard:** If you are in a discussion with your spouse and all of a sudden they are angry or upset and the conversation has taken a sharp turn in a direction that you didn't intend, it's often helpful to ask your spouse to repeat what you have just heard them say. Your spouse will say you just told him that he didn't do anything all day, when what you really said was, "What did you do today?" Now, what you said can be interpreted the way you said it, and it also can be interpreted differently. This is where it starts to get complicated. Have you said that same phrase in the past in a negative manner? Does your spouse feel like they didn't do anything all day? Context is everything, and that context changes, so it can be helpful to have your spouse repeat what you said to them if you feel like it was interpreted wrong. This will fairly quickly allow you to see where things got misinterpreted.
- **Don't Rush:** Communication is tricky and takes time. Don't rush discussion by trying to share important feelings at moments when they cannot be dealt with effectively. Couples will frequently have conversations when they are driving somewhere, only to have to pause those heavy conversations when they get to their destination. The same is true for bedtime. Laying down at night after a long day and then beginning to share your emotions with your spouse can have some disastrous effects, and that's true even if you don't fall asleep! I frequently have couples tell me that they will wait to have discussions at my office

because they go so much better when I'm in the room. I like the compliment, but often the conversation going well has more to do with it not being rushed. One of the main reasons a discussion goes so well in my office is because the couple has already made a number of choices that increase their chances of having a good discussion. They have set aside an hour to talk. Removed all distractions. They're sitting on a couch next to each other and want the situation fixed. You can do all of those things without a counselor!

- **Civility and respect:** Often, one of the best ways to improve communication is to talk to your spouse like you would an acquaintance or friend. You will treat them with respect, allow them to speak, and when you disagree, you're tactful and careful. **Unfortunately, we often talk to our spouses worse than we would talk to a stranger.** Not pretty, but true.

- **Negative Feedback:** Be careful with the comments you make when your spouse is communicating their feelings. Comments telling them they're wrong or mocking their feelings do nothing to further the discussion. Be careful of the comments you don't make as well. Silence can often be seen as negative.

Those are the basic skills when it comes to communication. Now we need to talk about what is being communicated.

Often what is being communicated are feelings. This is the connection that you and your spouse want. This is where couples get angry when communication doesn't go well. What are you trying to communicate to your spouse? There are several things you should be trying to speak to them about and a number of things you should not be communicating.

One big thing couples often get mixed up are "hurt" and "hate." I like to take some things to the extreme in my counseling sessions because it often helps couples see what they are doing. If they can understand what they are doing when it is exaggerated, they can begin to recognize it at a more subtle level.

I realize "hate" is more accurately expressed as "anger," but for the purpose of the illustration, it helps to think of this emotion as hate. Frequently you will be communicating hate when you should be communicating hurt. During an argument, you will be angry and tell your spouse how mean they are when you should really be sharing how hurt you are. Here's an example of a conversation where hurt and hate were confused:

Her: Why are you such a jerk?! You knew that I needed you to be home so I could go to the party with my friends. You only ever think about yourself! You're so selfish.

Him: I couldn't help it! What do you want me to do? Quit my job!? You never appreciate what I do for you and the family! You're the selfish one!

Now it's on! The fight will keep going with each person sharing the anger, or hate, they have for the other. If you can learn to communicate hurt instead of hate, the conversation will go much better. Here is an example of how this same conversation should look:

Her: I'm really frustrated that you didn't come home on time. I was really looking forward to going to the party with my friends.

Him: I'm sorry, I didn't mean to frustrate you. I got stuck at work, and I couldn't get away sooner. I know it was important to you. I was trapped, I couldn't get away for you and make my boss happy, too.

Do you see how much better that conversation goes when you can share hurt instead of hate? Your spouse will respond to what they see. If you can communicate hurt, that is what your spouse sees. Your spouse will react to the hurt. If your spouse sees hate first, that's what he will respond to.

A good example of responding to what you see is a child's reaction to getting hurt. What do you do when your child stubs her toe outside and comes running to you, crying? Typically you will sweep her up, cuddle her, and attend to her bleeding toe. You don't yell at your child and tell her you said not to go outside without shoes on! That greeting seems rude if your child is sharing hurt and you respond to her with anger.

The same is true for your spouse. What you show your spouse is what they will respond with. Communicate hurt, not hate.

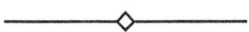

Sometimes communication is about communicating the right thing clearly, but there are also times when communication is about the small stuff that is easily missed. It's one thing to make sure you're communicating the right feelings, but you also need to be aware of the small little words, looks, and phrases that you're sharing because those "little things" have tons of power.

What are you trying to say when you're staring at the floor? What are you saying when you're huffing as your spouse speaks? What are you saying when you walk out of the room while your spouse is talking? Granted, that last one is not small, but it sends the same message as all the other supposedly small gestures. How would you expect your spouse to react if you walked out of the room while he was sharing his hurt? Do you give him the same space to react when you do some of the "small things" mentioned above? Communication is really tricky. It's even harder when you're mad. Sometimes there are so many tiny little signals occurring during one interaction that it's hard to separate what is being said and what is being received.

Small gestures can be helpful as well. They don't always need to be negative. Like when you share your feelings with your spouse and she reacts with moist eyes? That's a positive small gesture. She has heard you, she understands. What is being communicated when a spouse who was arguing with you just a minute ago responds with respectful silence? That's also a positive communication gesture.

Recognizing the small stuff and what is being communicated is one thing, but what do you do when what you see and hear are two different things? How do you handle the mixed messages? There will be times when what you are saying and what you are showing are two separate messages. How is your spouse supposed to know what to do? Which message do you believe when your spouse is sending two different messages at once?

The general rule here is to always believe the body language over the actual words. This is not always accurate, however. There are times, usually in fights, when your body language

Communication

will say that you don't like or believe something that is being said, but you're aware enough to know that it is probably true. You say you understand when clearly you don't, but you know that's the right answer, and you're trying to move the conversations forward. That is the healthy, correct thing to be doing in this situation, but right about that time your spouse will call you out on your body language that says otherwise, and now the argument just went backward.

Here's a story from me and my wife, Michelle, to further illustrate how this kind of mixed message communication can go down:

Michelle: Why can't you keep your clothes picked up in the bedroom?

Me: I don't know. I really don't care if they're on the floor.

Michelle: I have asked you a thousand times to please pick them up and not to throw them on the floor. Put them away or throw them in the laundry. I don't think you understand how much it stresses me out and frustrates me when I see your clothes all over the floor. You say you're going to pick them up and deal with them, but you don't.

Me: (Realizing that she is right, I do say that, and there are not any really significant changes in my behavior, I reluctantly reply) Okay, I'm sorry. (I still don't get why it's such a big deal that I leave my clothes on the floor and why it stresses her out so much. I don't get it, and that shows on my face when I'm telling her I'm sorry.)

Michelle: I still don't think you get it! (She isn't feeling heard at this moment. It's not about clothes. It's about why I wouldn't help her feel better. She correctly perceived that I don't get it.)

This is the crucial moment in the argument. The next response can make things go really bad or really good. You have to be able to see this spot right here. You need to know what to address: the circumstance or the feelings. I will show you both options since I have done them both! 😊

Me: What more do you want!? I said that I would try to do better. I can't say anything more than that.

Michelle: Well, I guess I will just have to learn to live with frustration at you!

Me: Well, I do it all the time! So welcome to the club!

Not cool. Mean, but real.

Here's how to keep this conversation from going downhill—changing from talking about the circumstance or the clothes to the feelings that are happening.

Michelle: I still don't think you get it!

Me: You're right. I honestly don't get it. My brain works differently than yours. Clothes on the floor don't register or bother me. I'm not trying to be dismissive of your feelings. I know it's a fair and reasonable request, I'm just not sure how good I will be at picking things up, and I know it frustrates you. I'm not trying to discourage you. I will try to do better at realizing how this impacts you. Please remember there are things that you do that frustrate and stress me out as well.

That answer takes a lot of practice, but it changes the dynamic of the argument to focus on the feelings that are going on.

Recognizing that there are dual messages happening simultaneously, in this case picking up clothes and not feeling heard and understood, and subsequently knowing which one to talk about first helps keep things at a point where you can continue talking to get through the conversation.

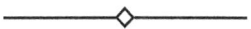

Dual messages are one thing. What do you do when you have multiple messages, more than two, coming at you at once? How do you separate out the truth?

Multiple messages usually come when you're in an argument. What do you do when your spouse says, "You are such a jerk! You never give me any credit for what I do for you. You are just selfish, and I don't know why anyone would be with you!"?

There's a lot of communication going on in those phrases. What happens if you stopped listening after that first sentence? Is that the feeling—that you're a jerk—the only thing your spouse was trying to communicate? What if you just heard the last thing your spouse said ringing in your head? Is that the feeling you think they were trying to communicate? What type of response do you think you're going to get if you call your spouse selfish or a jerk?

When you're in a situation where you're receiving a lot of messages at once, **can you sort through and find the feeling?** And not just the anger! Notice that the sentence in the middle of all the other stuff is the one that really matters here. If you just told your spouse, "You don't give me credit for all the things I do for you," I think the reaction would be different.

In terms of communication, you need to slow down and make sure you are communicating the feeling you want to communicate. If you add too many other things to your feelings, the feeling itself will get lost.

When you unload all those things at once like in the above statement, typically a spouse has two choices: believe everything you say or none of it. That is often why it will feel like your spouse is not listening to you. You will make a statement like the above, and your spouse will simply say, "I think you're just mad and don't really mean what you're saying." Now you feel like what you thought you shared is effectively discounted because of how it was framed. To have effective communication, you need to make sure you are sending one feeling at a time that your spouse can respond to. When listening, you need to be able to pull out the one feeling that is being communicated to you and not get sidetracked on the anger and frustration. Imagine how your spouse feels if your response to their outburst is not calling them a jerk or selfish too, but instead saying, "You're right, I don't always appreciate what you do for me." The whole tone of what is being communicated stays on task, and you are able to get closer to resolving the issue.

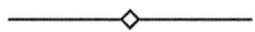

Those are a lot of the challenging things that happen while you're simply trying to convey to your spouse how you're feeling. How do you get around these pitfalls and avoid some of the arguments? Slow down and practice.

Don't try to communicate some of your biggest challenges and problems right off the bat, start with smaller everyday things. Get good at doing all the above and then you can start trying to communicate deeper and more powerful feelings. **Remember, communication is simply about getting your feelings across to your spouse.** Nothing more. Not whose feeling is right or better—simply what you're feeling.

> **COMMUNICATION IS SIMPLY ABOUT GETTING YOUR FEELING ACROSS TO YOUR SPOUSE.**

Sharing feelings is the essence of intimacy. Sharing feelings makes it feel like it's you and your spouse against the world. That is a great feeling. When it feels like it's you against the world that's horrible. This usually happens when your feelings are not being heard. So, keep practicing and going slow. Think about a conversation between you and your spouse that occurs frequently but is typically not done very well. I'm going to use a mild example here where there are usually not a lot of hurt feelings, but this example does illustrate some communication problems and how you can practice on smaller things. Here I present to you, the never-ending saga of ... where do you want to eat!?

This happens all the time when you and your spouse are finally ready to go out and have some time together. Your spouse asks where you want to eat. The exchange usually goes down like this:

Him: Where do you want to eat tonight?

Her: I don't know, where you do want to go?

Him: I don't care. I think I picked last time.

Her: No, you didn't pick. We used a gift card that we got for your birthday from work.

He: Yes, I used the gift card, and it was where I wanted to go. So it's your turn. Where do you want to eat?

Her: I don't know. What are you in the mood for?

Him: I'm up for about anything.

Her: Are you okay with Mexican?

Him: Sure, that sounds fine.

Her: What about seafood? We haven't had that in a while.

Him: Okay.

Her: Seriously, where do you want to go?

Him: I don't care, just pick a place.

Her: Why do you have to get so angry?

Him: I'm not angry, I just want to go eat.

Her: Well, I don't really care, just pick.

Him: Fine, we'll go with Mexican.

Her: Is that really what you want, or did you just pick that because I picked it?

Him: What do you mean you didn't pick anything? I had to. I always have to.

That exchange may be a little exaggerated, but it's pretty similar to what a lot of couples experience. And now that conversation is the beginning of your date night. How do you think the rest of the night will go?

Now, sometimes that whole encounter will be done in a light-hearted and fun mood, but sometimes it will be done in a frustrated mood. Other times one of you will be in a frustrated mood while the other is in a light-hearted mood. Either way, this conversation gives us a good example of how and how not to communicate.

WARNING: ASKING MORE QUESTIONS BEFORE ANSWERING THE ONE ASKED OF YOU IS NOT COMMUNICATION.

The first thing I want you to look at is how long this conversation was and how none of the questions were ever answered! Not one. Is that communicating? There are a lot of words being said and a lot of emotions trying to be conveyed, but I'm not sure there was any accurate communication going on. Go back and read only the female dialogue. Now go back and read only the male dialogue. Apply what we have already learned about communication to this conversation. Can you see all the errors? The biggest error here appears to be the very little listening and interaction going on. Both parties are being lazy, not taking any time to communicate their feelings. They are solely trying to hear what their spouse is saying, which means they are having their spouse do the work first. **Asking more questions before answering the one asked of you is not communication.**

Imagine how the tone of the conversations goes if instead of saying, "I don't know what to say," you said, "I don't want to pick tonight"? Can you feel the difference that happens when you just disclose more feelings in your answer? It may not solve the problem, he may respond that he doesn't want to pick either, but now at least you're communicating. You have both shared your indifference and the fact that you don't want to choose. That is much healthier than pretending to pick or trying to get your spouse to pick. You may end up in an argument, but at least it will be a genuine one about how you both are feeling—that neither one of you wants to pick where to eat. That fight is way easier to solve than personal attacks about never helping out or getting your way all the time. If you're sharing and communicating feelings, you will see later how that will make your fights easier to solve. Do you think it's easier to solve who always picks the restaurant, or is it easier to figure out what you should do when neither of you feels like picking a restaurant?

Next, look at how often in that conversation one spouse acknowledged the other spouse's perspective. Is the one spouse validated or allowed not to have an opinion on where they go to eat? Are they allowed to have that opinion? How come one spouse can have no preference, but it's a problem when the other spouse doesn't have an opinion? Too often, we are so caught up in our own side or opinion that we are trying to get across to our spouse that we miss what is being sent back at us. We're so busy trying to argue things that it becomes embarrassing or even hypocritical that we are missing it, all the while complaining that our spouse is not listening to us. Basically, you're saying, *I'm trying to tell you I have no opinion, but I'm mad that you have no opinion.* That is not a good look, but it happens often.

Finally, it's essential to remember that sometimes you will get into trouble for not communicating feelings even when the feelings are good ones. Often trying to be kind and friendly can cause communication errors. Trying to be the one who is flexible and let your spouse pick where they want to eat is a very nice and noble thought and idea. But not communicating that feeling is not helpful. Nowhere in that dialogue did either of the parties share that the reason they were not picking was because they were being kind and letting their spouse pick. Really cool and nice thoughts, but both of them missed that.

Communicate what you're thinking, then say that! I say that exact phrase hundreds of times in therapy. A spouse will tell me about an incident that happened and how it went sideways on them. He will typically end his story with the very thing he should have told his spouse at the beginning of the conversation. It usually sounds something like this:

Him: We went out for supper last night. I asked her where she wanted to go, she didn't answer and told me I needed to be a leader more in our relationship and take charge. I got angry with her and it ended in this big fight all over something stupid. I just wanted to take her to a place she liked because I had been gone most of the week and wanted to do something nice for her.

There it is, **just say that!** Say what you are thinking. People often get scared that saying what they're thinking will cause a fight or big argument. Typically if you don't say it, you will be in a fight anyway. Say what you're thinking in your head. It's usually not only what should be said, but also it's usually the feelings you're holding back. Remember, when you're communicating and thinking about something in your head, just say what's in there.

The next big tool when it comes to communication is knowing what you are trying to do or solve when communicating. **You are solving the problem, not your spouse's personality.** Trying to get your spouse to be different than who they are is not the way to communicate. Telling your spouse how you're feeling is more productive. When you're communicating, don't make the mistake of telling your spouse how they are wrong, mistaken, dumb, clueless, etc. Share the problem, tell your spouse what you're feeling, and then tell them what you need. That is way more productive. Tell her you need to feel appreciated, not that she is so selfish.

You and your spouse are going to be different. You are not meant to be the same, and your personalities are different, as we said earlier. Stop seeing changing the other person as the goal—the goal is to commit to educating them on seeing your side, not joining your side.

In premarital counseling, I will do an exercise with couples that lets them see how different they are and how different they think. I will ask them questions and tell them to not answer right away. I then give them a series of questions to answer. Some of the questions are as follows:

1. How much money do you need in your savings account to feel safe?

Communication

2. How often should you go to bed at the same time in a week?
3. What time is the ideal bedtime?
4. What time is the best time to get up in the morning?
5. How much money should you spend on a new car?
6. How often should you clean the house?
7. How often do you want to have sex in a week?

Now, what couples very quickly figure out when we are reviewing their answers is that **the numbers they give as answers don't match.** They never do. They initially think, oh no! We're in trouble because our numbers don't match! But as we work through the questions, they begin to see that this is an illustration showing them that communication is the goal, helping you learn how to articulate your feelings and understand that your spouse is different from you. The goal is not to get your spouse to pick your number, the goal is for them to know why your number is important to you. Once you get there, then you can begin to compromise or figure out how to navigate the difference between your numbers. The other point with these questions is to help couples realize that all throughout life, the numbers won't match, and to remember that this is never the problem. You will see this phrase repeated plenty of times throughout this manual: Your numbers don't match. Remember that is not the problem.

Typically when you figure out that your numbers don't match, you will try to over-explain why you chose the number you did. Don't use too many words when doing this. It will cause the communication to get sidetracked and can quickly turn into an argument. Keep it straightforward. **Bold but simple.**

BOLD BUT SIMPLE

Here's an illustration from a couple who used too many words and had a pattern of making communication harder than it already is:

BEN AND LESLIE.

Ben and Leslie have only been married for two years. They were fighting quite a bit and could never get anything resolved. They didn't like to fight, and when they did, it would go round and round for hours until they gave up said they didn't want to fight anymore and just moved on. Ben and Leslie would frequently get into a disagreement while in counseling. Most likely the arguments would have gotten bigger if I had not been in the room. I asked each of them what they needed from their spouse. Ben and Leslie always did the same thing when asked this question: They would verbalize what they needed from their spouse in the first sentence of their response. After the first sentence, they would go on to give examples and reasons why they were feeling a certain way. Then their partner would respond by defending themselves. The other spouse would defend against the blame, but then forget or never address the need that their spouse had expressed early on in the conversation. It looked like this:

Leslie: I need you to be more supportive and helpful to me. You always make a big production and act like what I'm asking you to do is so complicated and challenging. Like it's unreasonable and a big inconvenience that I ask you for help.

Ben: I only overreact because you're always asking me to do things when you never do anything for me. You simply try to use me to do stuff you don't want to do or didn't get done, and you don't ever help me when I ask for help with things.

Leslie: When did you ask me to do something that I didn't do for you? I do stuff for you all the time! Didn't I make supper for you yesterday? I do a hundred things for you, and you never do anything for me!

Ben: What do you mean I never do anything for you? I just finished painting the downstairs bedroom for you last weekend. I didn't want to paint it, but you said it needed to be painted, so it did it!

Did you notice what happened? Ben never acknowledged Leslie's request about being supportive and helpful. After this conversation, when Ben was done venting his frustration, I simply asked him if he was open to helping out his wife more. He replied immediately, "Well yeah, who wouldn't be willing to help out their wife?" I told him then tell her that! Remember the "then say that!" phrase.

Most of this fight could have been avoided if Leslie just used fewer words. What happens if she just says the first sentence: "I need you to be more supportive and helpful to me"? Ben and Leslie would most likely not argue about supper and painting if the only thing Ben responds to is Leslie's request for help. This is an excellent example of how fast an argument can occur and how adding too many words when expressing

The Marriage Manual

feelings can cause things to be confusing. Learning how to slow down and communicate feelings takes practice.

An initial homework assignment that I give couples is a communication exercise designed to help foster communication despite each person's different personalities. When a couple comes in for therapy, I typically try to get them to be better communicators regardless of the situation that is occurring. One way I do this is by having the couple talk about me and what they thought about the first session of therapy. It's a good topic to communicate about because it's fresh, and they typically have not had a lot of fights about me ...yet! (☺). I tell them to go home and talk about me, what they thought of therapy, and if they want to return. Sounds simple enough, right? They usually say yes, and that's it. If I let them leave at this point, they would probably do the same thing they always do. It would go something like this:

Her: Well, what did you think of therapy?

Him: I don't know, what did you think of therapy?

Her: Well, I thought it went okay. It wasn't too bad, and it wasn't as awkward as I thought.

Him: Yeah, I agree, it wasn't too bad.

Her: I thought he did a good job talking to both of us.

Him: Uh-huh.

Her: He also seemed to have a good plan on what we can do to make this better.

Him: Yep.

Her: I thought he would have asked more about our history and want to get to know us better. I didn't think he really took the time to learn about us and the things that brought us into counseling. I hope we can get into that later. He didn't give us any homework to do other than talk about him. I wonder if that will always be like that? I don't know, but I think I can give it a chance and I would like to go back, what do you think?

Him: Sounds good.

Her: What else? Now it's your turn to go! What did you think about counseling?

Him: I already told you it was good.

Her: How are we ever going to get any better if you don't participate and try? If you don't try, this is not going to work!

What just happened? Do you know what went wrong? How did this end up in a fight?

When I give this assignment to couples, I tell them a few things other than to just go home and talk about therapy. I ask them to make sure they communicate feelings, not just facts. Facts do not provide any guidance of how well connected you are to someone. Sharing observations of what my office was like or what I was wearing does nothing to convey how you felt about attending counseling, so stay away from that. It will just add distractions.

The second thing I do is find out who uses the most words in the relationship and who is more in touch with their feelings. This is typically the female, but not always. The person who uses the most words in the relationship cannot go first in this exercise. (They typically always do.) The person who uses the most words and has the most feelings will typically go first in this kind of conversation because that's their personality, and they feel the most comfortable doing so. They will take charge and do a great job of saying what they thought and how they felt. They may have reasons and examples that they share. They will pour out their heart and then look over at their spouse, expecting the same thing in return—sharing thoughts and feelings and this great exchange of emotions—and they will simply get a "sounds good" or "me too."

Now the wife feels like she is doing all the work and her husband is not engaged. Guess what, you're right. That is precisely what happened. You just took all the answers that the person with fewer words has, and they have nothing to add, so they say nothing. For context, what is usually going on in the man's head while his wife is talking is typically very helpful if he would just say what he was thinking. Typically he doesn't have many words or feelings on this example. He may simply feel that it was not too bad and the therapist was a nice guy. He felt comfortable and is willing to go back. Those are nice, solid feelings with not a lot of extra, but his personality is to wait to talk to see what others say. So he defers to his wife, and she starts on her side. He listens, sees how they tend to have the same views, and thinks things are good. Then she keeps talking and starts bringing up something he had not even thought about, feelings that never even crossed his mind. He quickly sees that she has thought this through much more than he has and she is clearly more advanced in her thinking on this matter, so he decides to follow her lead.

Really cool thought, but what comes out of his mouth is usually only "sounds good." And the fight is on.

If you make the person who uses fewer words go first, the outcome is way better. It takes a little training for the man to take the risk and go first. It takes a little practice to make sure the wife goes second, but when they do communication is much better, and the connection is more substantial. When you communicate from of a place of knowing your personalities and abilities, you can improve your communication. Here is how the conversation should go when done differently:

Her: We need to do the assignment from the therapist. Are you ready to talk about it?

Him: Sure.

Her: Okay, remember you need to go first?

Him: That's right, what was I supposed to talk about again?

Her: What you liked about counseling and if you want to come back.

Him: Oh yeah. Well, it wasn't too bad. I thought it was going to be worse.

Her: Anything else?

Him: He seemed to be fair. I'd go back. What did you think?

Her: I liked him too. I agree it wasn't too bad. It wasn't as awkward as I thought. He was fair. He did a good job of talking to both of us. I thought he would have asked more about our history and want to get to know us better. I didn't think he really took the time to learn about us and the things that brought us into counseling. I hope we can get into that later. He didn't give us any homework to do other than talk about him. I wonder if that will always be like that? I don't know, but I think I can give it a chance and I would like to go back too.

Do you hear the difference in that conversation? Did you notice that it's almost all of the same words as the first one? The only difference the second time around is that the couple is communicating together. That's a good example of how just a few small changes can really help communication grow. The husband used more words and participated, and the wife felt like she was not alone and doing the assignment by herself. I will tell couples that they should practice and use this technique often, especially if they have a big decision to make as a couple.

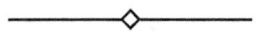

Hopefully, your communication is getting a little better by using this tool correctly. Keep practicing communicating on various things, and don't start with the most challenging issues first. Practice communicating about easy topics and subjects. Once you get better at that, I want to make sure you know how to communicate that you love each other. One of the best ways to do this is by knowing what your love language is. *The Five Love Languages* by Gary Chapman is an excellent book[3]. I highly recommend it. Many couples have heard about it, but here's a quick synopsis.

There are five different ways people feel loved. They are all great, but one will speak to you more than the others. The

---

[3]Chapman, Gary. *The Five Love Languages: How to Express Heartfelt Commitment to your Mate.* Northfield Publishing, 2004.

five different love languages are words of affirmation, touch, quality time, gifts, and acts of service. Like we talked about earlier, you and your spouse most likely won't have the same love language. Remember, numbers don't match! We tend to give love using the love language we want, not necessarily the one that our spouse needs. When you want to show your spouse you love them, you have to think like them and try to use the love language they need. That's my short summary, but it's an excellent book, go check it out.

But in terms of communication, you should know how your spouse feels most loved and valued. You will need to talk and communicate to find this out. This should be a fun task, not a damaging fight. Remember all the communication techniques you want to be able to discover and use to learn how to love your spouse. Take some time and practice your communication tool by finding out how your spouse feels most loved before proceeding.

Before we close out this section on communication, here's one more example of knowing what you're communicating about. Before you end up in a fight, make sure you are at least fighting about the same thing.

SAM AND REBECCA.

Rebecca: I want a convertible. He never wants to spend any money. He never lets me have anything I want.

Therapist: Do you want your wife to have a convertible?

Sam: Well, I would like a new truck too, but it will cost too much money. She doesn't understand that there are lots of things I want to have, but I'm not able to have. She thinks that

I just don't let her buy anything. We don't have the money to do everything she wants. If I didn't tell her not to buy something as much as I do, we would never have money for anything. She doesn't understand that we need to make sacrifices so we can be secure.

Therapist: Do you want your wife to have a convertible?

Sam: Well, of course, but we can't afford that now.

Therapist: Tell your wife.

Sam: I did.

Therapist: Tell your wife that you would like it if she could have a convertible.

Sam: I would like you to have a convertible.

Therapist: Great. Now both of you pause for a second and let that sink in. Now you guys can talk about your finances and what plans you guys want to make.

After Rebecca hears that Sam is not against her having a convertible, solving the problem becomes much more manageable. They can now talk and figure out if this purchase is possible. Will they have to wait a year? What is their plan to save money? Did Sam think that this convertible would be in addition to her other car? Was Rebecca willing to sell her current car and get a used one? They may not be able to go get a convertible right after the session, but if they are on the same page, talking becomes much more comfortable. Learning how to communicate about the same thing at the same time will take some practice.

START FROM A PLACE YOU AGGREE ON

What I mean by starting from a place where you agree is this: All adults have different parenting styles. One parent may think that it is best to be firm and strict, another parent may think it is best to be more of a gentle teacher. When a child misbehaves, the couple will argue about whose way is the best and how the other person's way is wrong. What is the best way to handle a child who is talking back and being disrespectful? Give them a consequence for their actions? Tell them why talking back is wrong and how it can hurt people or get them in trouble? Couples will spend a lot of time arguing about their approach to this parenting choice. I want the couple to start from a place where they agree.

Clearly, both parents have a view of wanting their child to be respectful of others and not talk back. Neither one of them would argue about that not being important. It's a lot easier to communicate about how you would teach respect as opposed to fighting because you believe your spouse doesn't care what you think.

Another great example is kids and their music. Parents will always come in and tell me how bad the music their kids are listening to is. The parents typically keep trying to shut down what their kids are doing, and the kid is fighting back. Start on the common ground, then communicate. I will ask the parent if their mom or dad liked the music they listened to.

Typically they didn't. I slow the parent down and have them remember what that feeling was like and the frustration they had about their mom or dad never listening to them. I then spend some time talking with the kid, helping them figure out what their parent is worried about. They usually say something along the lines of their parent not thinking their music is appropriate. I then ask the kid where they think the line is between appropriate and inappropriate. Often they're so busy fighting with their parent that they have never expressed what they think is inappropriate in music. They usually do have a line, it's just different from their parents' line. Having the kid say what they believe is too much or is inappropriate helps free up communication and finding a compromise. Start where you agree, not where you disagree.

Remember that in communication, you are two different people with different feelings and thoughts trying to communicate those thoughts and feelings. Often you are both trying to communicate those things at the same time. You can be an effective communicator, but if you are both communicating at the same time, trouble is brewing. If you are communicating your feelings at the same time and you both think you're talking about the same thing but you're not, we now have a fight.

Communication

— NOTES —

— NOTES —

— TOOL #3 —

KNOW HOW TO FIGHT

The next tool you need to have for a healthy marriage is knowing how to fight. When I'm talking about fighting, I'm not talking about actual physical fighting, but instead arguing or disagreeing—being mad at each other. Whatever words you want to use, fighting is the act of disagreeing with one another. Sometimes it's intense, and sometimes it's not as fierce. Many couples fight, but very few of them know how to fight correctly.

First, we need to fix the myth that fighting in a marriage is wrong. It's not. Some couples will actually proudly tell me that they never fight. They are usually sitting in marriage therapy when they are saying that! Fighting is seen as negative and bad. Think for a minute about what it means if you and your spouse never fight. I interpret that lack of fighting as either being married to a perfect person, or that you guys lie to each other a lot. You either never do anything wrong, or you lie when your spouse asks if anything is wrong. Obviously, having a relationship built on lies is not a good thing. We already learned that "your numbers don't match," so it's inevitable that a disagreement is going to occur, and you better know how to handle it.

ROSS AND RACHEL.

This couple has been married for three years. They dated for two years before they got married. Ross and Rachel came into counseling, and they were increasingly getting more and more annoyed with each other as the session went on. Both Ross and Rachel shared how their spouse was making them more irritated and driving them crazy.

Interestingly, they could identify what they were doing and not really blame the other person, but they both acknowledged that what they were doing was frustrating the other. Some of the stories they shared pointed to a history of not finishing fights. There was a lot of built-up frustration that was coming out in these annoyances.

I asked Ross and Rachel to tell me about the last fight they had. Rachel shared a story of how Ross came home and was upset that she was looking at her iPad. He was mad that the kitchen was a mess and she wasn't cleaning it. Ross said some mean things to Rachel. Rachel was angry because she had just sat down after spending a couple hours doing laundry and cleaning the bathrooms. Rachel then unloaded on Ross about how unappreciative he is and how he never gives her compliments and simply criticizes her. Ross responded by saying Rachel has so much free time since she only works part-time and she can't even get done the few things that he asks of her. Here's what happened next:

Therapist: How big did that fight get?

Rachel: I don't think we talked for the rest of that night? Right?

Ross: No, we didn't talk till bedtime the next evening. Over 24 hours.

Rachel: Yeah, that sounds about right.

Therapist: How did it finally end?

Rachel: We just ended it and moved on?

Ross: Yeah, that night we just said we were sorry and went to bed.

Therapist: How did you end it?? What does "move on" mean?

Ross: I told her I was sorry for yelling at her ...

Rachel: And I told him I was sorry for overreacting.

Therapist: Sounds like you apologized for your behaviors while you were fighting, but you didn't do anything else. What did you guys do to fix the problem, so it doesn't happen again?

Together: Nothing really.

Ross: I get so sick of fighting that I just want it to be over and move on. I hate how long it takes for us to apologize.

Rachel: I can say some mean things and feel bad for what I said when I was mad, so I want to just move on.

Therapist: If you don't take some time to talk about the incident that caused the fight, you will repeat it. I'm glad that you apologized for your actions when fighting, but you need to go back and talk about the feelings that were initially expressed. You guys never figured out Ross's expectations of what needs to get done around the house and whose responsibility it is.

You also never resolved Rachel's feelings about often feeling criticized. What resolutions did you come up with? That's why the fight keeps happening. Do that long enough and have enough fights over time and you will feel as though your spouse doesn't care and isn't trying. That is why over time you can get more and more annoyed with each other.

This couple was really good at apologizing and getting back to life, but not at dealing with things. If your solution to a fight is to say sorry for fighting and your spouse says me too, this is not the end of the fight—it's just the beginning of figuring out a solution.

I think the reason so many people don't know how to fight correctly is because they never had role models in this area. Think about your parents growing up. Our parents usually fall into one of two categories: They either fought all the time in front of the kids the wrong way, or they rarely fought in front of the kids. Couples always say that they never want to fight in front of their kids. While that's great in theory and avoiding fighting in front of the children as much as possible is a good thing, I want you to teach your kids how to fight correctly.

Think about how many times you would see some emotion erupt out of one of your parents, and then one of them would walk off. What happened next? Usually, the kids are sent to their rooms, or if it's bedtime, the kids are told to go to bed. You go to your room, go to bed, sleep, and get up the next morning. You come downstairs, and there are your parents magically doing well again. What happened? What did they do? How did they fix that? If you've never seen healthy fighting, it's not very likely that you'll be able to replicate healthy fighting when you get older.

So first we need to get over this idea that fighting is bad. Fighting is necessary for a marriage, you just need to do it differently. The old way of fighting is bad. Before we get going on the new way of fighting, you should know what the old way looks like. If you're not sure, go back to Tool #1. Learn about you. Part of your work should be to identify what you're like when you're angry. What do you say? How do you act? Do you get loud and shout, or do you get quiet and cold? I like to call these two different fighting attitudes "shouting" or "Siberia." You should know how you act.

If you're angry and your spouse walks into the room, how do they know you're mad? Is it loud and cupboards are shutting hard as you angrily unload the dishwasher? Is really quiet, and when your spouse asks what's wrong you simply say, "nothing, I'm fine" when you're clearly not fine?

You better know what you need when you are mad. Do you need space and time to think, or do you need to solve the problem right away? How has the way you handled anger in the past affected your fights? Basically, what is your old way of fighting? We want to be aware of that when we're using this new tool of fighting in a healthy manner.

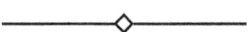

The ABC's. We're going to go over the **ABC's of fighting**. Then I will spend some time with a few examples and specifics, much like we did with Tool #2.

The ABC's are just that: A-Anger. A fight usually starts with the sharing of anger. B- Break. You will need to take a break because the sharing usually gets too fast and intense, and the C- Conclusion. How did the fight end? What was the resolution?

Let's look at each of these ABC's in a little more detail.

A

Anger. Most fights involve anger. In this new, healthy way of fighting, you will need to learn how to remove anger from the situation. Anger gets in the way and makes the whole thing way too hard to handle. Why is anger even there in the first place? A fight is really about two different sides of something. Where does the anger come from? Usually, anger comes from trying to communicate your side and feeling like you haven't been heard or that you've been discounted.

Remember the lessons we learned from Tool #2: Communication—communicate by sharing the hurt, not the hate. Remember to separate the anger from what you are trying to say. If you are trying to say that you're angry, then say that—don't show, demonstrate, or describe it. Remember, you're not very articulate when you're angry. If your spouse is angry, they're not good at listening. If you're communicating when you're angry, it will be almost impossible to do so effectively. This is what I mean when I say you're not a good communicator.

When you're angry you will say things like, "You never listen to me," "You always get your way" or, "You never say you're sorry." I'm guessing you know what happens when you make these statements—your spouse tells you that saying she never does something or she always acts a certain way are not true, and now you're arguing about how what you said was wrong and they miss what you were actually trying to get across to them. If you are not able to remove the anger, very little productive communication will occur. If you are not able to see the other person's side, you're in trouble.

I will often ask couples to tell me about a big fight they had. As soon as I'm sure they are both thinking about the same incident, I stop them from talking about it. Then I make them fight the incident backward. Meaning the husband has to tell me what message the wife was trying to get across to him, and the wife has to say to me what message the husband was trying to get across to her. They usually get it partly right. The couple is so busy trying to make their individual point that often they are missing what the other person is trying to say in the process. If you don't know what your spouse is trying to get across to you, it's time to take a break.

Why is the person who says she loves you and cares for you yelling and being mean? It's your job to figure that out. The old way of fighting would be to tell her she is being mean and maybe even point out how mean she is. I want you to think differently. I want you to ask yourself, *How did your spouse get hurt? What role did you play in that?* You may have hurt your spouse intentionally, but most likely the hurt was unintentional. If you're not in a spot to figure this out, take a break.

If you can't communicate your feelings without anger, if you can't figure out what your spouse is trying to tell you, if you can't figure out why your spouse is hurting you—and most importantly—**if you're convinced that you are right and she is wrong ... TAKE A BREAK!**

 **MARRIAGES MAY OVERHEAT, TAKE A BREAK**

B|

Break. Breaks are called many things: timeouts, pause, rest, etc. It doesn't matter what you call it, you must take one if things are going too fast. If you don't take a break, things will escalate,v and they will sometimes escalate very quickly.

Taking a break sounds nice and straightforward. But it's usually tough and actually takes years of practice to get good at. Why is taking a break during a fight so hard? Mainly because we're different people from our spouse and the things that get us upset and hurt us are different. Remember, "your numbers don't match." Meaning the two of you have different personalities and different things that will hurt you.

How this shows up in taking a break is you will often have one person in the relationship who loves to take breaks and probably takes them too often, where the other person in the relationship never wants to take a break and simply wants to power through to finish the argument. This is a common problem, and this situation has been described in several different ways. There are actually a number of phrases for the phenomenon: pursuer/distance, or I have also heard it described as a turtle and a rabbit. They all mean the same thing. Which one are you when it comes to taking a break? (If you don't know, refer back to Tool #1.) What this means practically is taking a break is hard because one person likes to take the break and doesn't want to come back to address the heart of the fight, while the other person is so worried that the fight will never get solved that they won't take the break. This concept is probably best illustrated by my own poor behaviors when I was first married:

When I was first married and my wife and I would have a fight, it would not be pretty. I'm the type of person who wants to solve the fight right away and get things back to feeling normal. We would get into an argument and I would keep talking and arguing and ignore my wife's requests to take a break. I would keep going until she was overwhelmed. She would then run to our bedroom and slam the door. When that happened I would sit there with my mind racing and think, Oh no, we need to resolve this, this is getting worse, a marriage with unresolved conflict is not good. So I would go into the bedroom and continue what I thought was a healthy, problem-solving solution to the fight, i.e. I would tell her how upset I was. Well, guess what happened when I walked in and started doing this? Yep, you guessed it, she got up and went into the bathroom to keep avoiding me.

What do you think I did next? Remember, I'm thinking the world is ending, and we need to solve this, and I'm a slow learner! I opened the bathroom door and what happens? My wife is now stuck in a room with me and very angry. She proceeds to tell me every bad thing I've done since we have been married and why I'm such a bad person, then she runs out of the house and goes for a drive.

How do you think I'm feeling now? If I was worried about how we were doing before, I'm pretty much going crazy now. This fight also happened back in the time when we didn't have cell phones (dating myself here), so I couldn't even text my wife 300 times! (Probably good I wasn't able to do that.) But I need to finish the story.

After my wife took her break, she came back and we talked through things and everything was resolved. I later went back and asked why she had been so mean and left me hanging when she ran to the bedroom and then went for a drive. She explained that she had heard all the things I was saying, and she needed some time to think about whether I was right or fair in what I was saying. She needed time to think about what her role was in the situation and how she wanted to respond to me. She didn't want to just say mean things back. (In my head I was thinking, *If that was what you were doing, take all the time you need!*).

I told my wife that her explanation was very helpful, but it would have been even more helpful if she had told me that in the first place because that wasn't what I thought was going on in the moment. She then proceeded to ask me what I had been thinking when she drove off. I told her how scared I was that our marriage was not going well and that it felt like everything was falling apart. She then said something I will never forget: "Why were you so worried? I just needed a break. I will always come back."

We've been married for 27 years now and we're getting really good at taking breaks. Now when we fight and she says I need a break, I stop the fight right away. Her breaks usually only take 30 seconds, not 30 minutes, and we move on with the argument.

That is the secret to breaking the cycle of a fight to take a successful break: knowing that you will get a chance to continue the discussion. If you never come back and address the issue after a break, it won't work. If you never reassure your spouse that you will resolve things, you won't get a break, and it won't work. Sometimes it's not pretty, but you must communicate that you will be back and the issue will be addressed. It's often not polite or articulate to say you need a break since you're sharing while you're angry. Telling your spouse that you need a break and that you will come back later and resolve the issue rarely sounds that eloquent. It often merely sounds like, "I can't stand you right now, and I will deal with you later!" Not nice, but effective. As long as your spouse knows that you will be back to resolve things, they will have a better chance at waiting to do so until after the break is over.

If you're the spouse who likes things resolved and has a hard time waiting, listen to the positive in that statement: you will get a chance to resume the conversation. This process may take a number of times, meaning you may have to have a few breaks, but hopefully, eventually, you can solve the problem.

C |

Conclusion. If you are able to take breaks and come back to listen to each other, you need to make sure you know what

SHARE HOW YOU GOT HURT, NOT WHO HURT YOU

to do next. Conclusion is the resolution of the argument. It has two parts: one is hearing the feelings of your spouse, and the second is making a plan to address, fix, or reduce whatever the fight was initially about. Learning what to say when you come back can help you resolve the fight faster without needing as many breaks. Why did you need a break? On the flip side, why did you feel like there was danger and you needed to resolve the issue right then and there? Earlier, we talked about sharing the hurt, not the anger, now when you're in a fight, you need to learn to **share HOW you got hurt, not WHO hurt you.**

A spouse tends to listen to you better when they're hearing *how* you got hurt instead of hearing that *they* hurt you. What would you rather hear: "Can I tell you how mean and stupid you are?" or, "Can you help me with the hurt I have from you?" The difference between sharing how you are hurt versus who hurt you can eliminate a lot of unnecessary arguing. If you're focused on sharing stuff based on how your spouse is mean, it tends to be a very short conversation and not that hard to do—making statements like, "You're annoying and you don't listen to me." It's short, easy, and allows your spouse to say the same thing right back at you. Saying, "I got hurt when you said this because it makes me feel like I'm never good enough, and I have a hard time believing I'm good enough," confirms some of your fears and takes a lot longer to say, sure. But it also invites a discussion that's not a fight and moves you towards the conclusion faster.

Do the work; don't fight with your spouse in a lazy manner.

When you share about how you got hurt, remember how you're sharing—if your "sharing" looks more like attacking, you might not be doing it right. Sharing how you got hurt should not sound or look like you're attacking your spouse. If you can't share without attacking them, go back and take a break. If you attack your spouse long enough, they will take the break for you.

Remember that sometimes this whole exchange will happen backward—you will hear the hurt. So, how are you hearing this hurt? Do you hear it as your spouse simply sharing hurt, or are you feeling attacked and becoming defensive? You need to be able to hear what your spouse is saying even if they're not very good at separating the *how* they got hurt with the *who* hurt them.

Defensiveness and withdrawal are the usual responses here, but they're not very helpful. Sometimes you need to be able to let stuff go that isn't important to your goal of hearing their hurt.

At times your spouse will be sharing how they got hurt with how you're mean sprinkled in. If you only keep responding to how you're not mean, you will escalate the fight and need to take more breaks. If you can learn to listen for the right things after the break in the argument, the argument will begin to resolve much faster.

Most of the time, the theme is about reassurance or connectedness. That feeling of, are we still okay? Am I still safe and loved? It's weird to think about how often that feeling will show up in life. Remembering what the theme is and what you're fighting about will help the efficiency of your fighting. If you think you're fighting about whether you're loved and valued but your spouse thinks you're fighting about something small like why you stayed out so late, the two of you will have very different reactions to the fight. If one of you is thinking you're fighting about marital commitment and the other thinks you're fighting about coming home an hour late, this conversation is not going to go well at all. Remembering that it is usually the little things that trigger the big feelings can help you pause and slow down so you don't need to do so much damage to each other before you figure out you need to pause.

The next step in working towards a conclusion in a fight is knowing the topic—know what you're fighting about. Frequently we think we are fighting about one thing when in reality we are fighting about something entirely different. On the surface most arguments are about little stuff, but they tend to have a bigger theme or meaning behind them. The underlying theme is usually more significant than the actual topic.

MAKE USE OF THE CRAP YOU HAVE BEEN THROUGH

Most of the time, the theme is about reassurance or connectedness. That feeling of, are we *still* okay? *Am I still safe and loved?* It's weird to think about how often that feeling will show up in life. Remembering what the theme is and what you're fighting about will help the efficiency of your fighting. If you think you're fighting about whether you're loved and valued but your spouse thinks you're fighting about something small like why you stayed out so late, the two of you will have very different reactions to the fight. If one of you is thinking you're fighting about marital commitment and the other thinks you're fighting about coming home an hour late, this conversation is not going to go well at all. Remembering that it is usually the little things that trigger the big feelings can help you pause and slow down so you don't need to do so much damage to each other before you figure out you need to pause.

Since fights are often about the little things, they can be paused. Once you both realize you're not talking about life and death issues in marriage but instead a small thing about when you came home, the fight can be paused until your anger and frustration levels go down.

As you get better at going through these steps when you fight, you will get faster, and in turn they will be less emotionally volatile. As a result you will go through the normal disagreements and hurts you inflict on each other much quicker. **Make use of the crap you have been through.** If you've been sharing your feelings with your spouse and have effectively resolved things 10 times, feel confident when number 11 comes along. Imagine if you have had this same disagreement 100 times or even 1,000 times. Things should not feel so desperate if you've already had this same fight a number of times already.

One thing that helps me when I'm in the middle of an argument with my wife is reminding myself, *Where are you going to be sleeping tonight?* The same place that I always do: next to my wife. Meaning, I'm mad right now, but I will calm down. We will share our hurt, find a resolution, and move on. We've done this argument a number of times, and we will do it a number more.

Find a resolution. If you've completed all the steps up until now, you should have had a fight, taken a break, shared your hurt, heard your spouse's hurt, and now you need to resolve or problem solve. If you've done these steps well, the resolution is usually pretty easy to come by.

Now it's time for resolution or compromise—what are you going to change to fix whatever caused the hurt in the first place? If you're having trouble getting to the resolution, this means you need to go back and do the steps again. When you're in the resolution phase, it should now be "we" solving the problem, not simply "me" or "you" by yourself. If you're still talking like your spouse needs to change or needs to be better, you're not at the resolution phase yet.

Walk through the example of a husband staying out too late. If the wife has shared how she was worried, angry, and felt disrespected by her husband staying out too late and he heard where those feelings were coming from and acknowledged them, and if the husband shared how his not coming home on time was not a reflection of how much he loves his wife, but simply not paying attention to the time and she has heard and understood him, then figuring out how to fix this problem of what to do when the husband goes out again becomes really easy.

The couple may more definitively decide what time to come home next time. They may decide that they need to talk and text more during the evening when one of them is out. The husband now knows that his goal is to make sure his wife is feeling respected and loved. The wife knows that her goal is to find out what his plans are and make the solution easier. As long as they are working together to seek out a compromise, this solution will not lead to a fight. If they do not work together, things quickly go back to an argument.

Resolution of the issue is the goal, not changing your spouse's personality. If the fight goes back to, "he should be more responsible with his time" or, "she should just learn to get over things," we have gone backward again. That is not what you're trying to fix here.

You're simply trying to fix when to come home. That's easy. Fixing people is really hard.

Make sure that when you're working on the resolution to an argument, you compromise. Most couples don't compromise. That sounds crazy, but they don't. In fact, they usually do the opposite of compromise. Most couples do all-or-nothing.

You'll hear this all-or-nothing attitude all too often if you listen for it. It comes out in phrases like, "Fine, whatever. You always have to have your way," or, "Okay, I'll never go out again." It doesn't even have to be done in a mean manner. Sadly, couples that really care for each other also don't tend to compromise. Sometimes those bad habits of not learning how to compromise can be done out of caring. We say things like, "I don't care, whatever you want," or, "It really doesn't matter to me. I know you want to do that, so it's fine."

If you don't compromise, you tend to start feeding resentment. Resentment can build and get in the way when you're trying to find a compromise next time. You'll feel angry, and you'll often hear things like, "We did it your way last time, it's my turn to win for once." Those types of statements don't sound like a compromise, do they?

Rember the numbers don't match lesson? Here's where the importance of understanding compromise comes in. Imagine a wife who's answering this question: How much money do you want in your savings account to feel safe? She answers, "$100."

Ask her husband the same question and his answer is, "$1,000." Now, imagine if this couple never communicates. He keeps trying to get more and more money into their savings account, and she keeps spending it because she feels like they have plenty. This lack of communication will cause plenty of fights—she will think he's a penny pincher, and he will think she's irresponsible with money. As soon as they talk and come to a compromise/resolution, things get easier. If they talk and agree together to keep $500 in their savings account, not only does the fighting stop, but also so does the resentment.

In a compromise, you should be able to say what you kept for yourself. This sounds selfish, but if you can't identify what you kept for yourself in a compromise, it means you probably didn't have a healthy, fair compromise. Once you know that you've been heard and you realize through fighting/discussion that things could be different, you're able to feel like your spouse has heard, and even taken into account, how you feel. This compromise over the savings account is also a good example of solving the problem, not the personality. We're solving how much money to save, not whose amount is better. Remember when you're resolving a fight, make sure you can identify the compromise.

Here is an example of a couple who struggled mightily to illustrate some of the stuff we just covered:

PAUL AND JAMIE.

Paul and Jamie would frequently argue about sex. Paul was frustrated because he felt like Jamie didn't like sex and didn't want to have it as much as he did. He would frequently argue with his wife about how she didn't want to have sex. Paul shared that Jamie would often turn him down and tell him that they would do it later. Paul was also irritated that when they did have sex, it was not spontaneous and exciting. Jamie was frustrated because Paul never thought about her or how she was feeling. He would frequently ask her for sex when she was tired or had several stressful things that she needed to get accomplished. Jamie enjoyed sex when they had it and didn't understand why Paul was not more sensitive to what she had going on.

Remember the things that you just read about fighting. The ABC's: A-The anger is pretty easy to figure out here, especially when talking about sex as almost all couples will get hurt when it comes to sex at some point. B-The break was not described, but Paul and Jamie had fought about this issue frequently and taken many breaks. C- Conclusion, can you figure out what this fight is about? Paul and Jamie initially couldn't. Paul thought the fight was about the fact that his wife didn't want to have sex. Jamie thought it was about Paul being insensitive to her needs. The fight was not about whether the couple wants to have sex, but when to have sex.

The compromise comes in once Paul and Jamie are able to start from a place where they both say they like sex and enjoy having it with each other. Knowing that Paul wants sex to be more spontaneous and Jamie wants sex to be scheduled, the compromise becomes clear. They decided that they would have one planned sexual encounter and one spontaneous encounter each week. The compromise allows for both to be understood and meet each other's needs. By working through the compromise, Paul and Jamie are no longer fighting over whether they are going to have sex, when they are going to have sex, or whose way of doing sex is better, instead they're focusing on how to compromise, which sidesteps needless arguments about things that were not the real issue.

I know that fighting is not fun, but is a necessary tool if you're going to have a healthy relationship. Finally, remember that it's been said many times that you can never prevent a fight from happening, but you can in fact avoid or postpone a fight for a long time. But the longer you postpone a fight, the bigger and more challenging it will be to solve.

— NOTES —

— NOTES —

— TOOL #4 —

GRACE

 **APPLY IT LIBERALLY TO ALL AREAS**

This tool is best used after you've seen it in action. It's even better if this tool of grace has been used on you. If grace has been used on, you will be better able to understand its power and how to use it adequately and correctly. If you have no experience with grace, it will be extremely difficult to apply in your marriage. There are going to be times where you're hurt, deserve better, and are owed more than you're getting from your spouse. When these times come, your marriage will get stuck, bogged down, and even feel hopeless. If you do not use this tool of grace, your marriage will sink into a nasty situation where you and your spouse are keeping score, and you will always feel like you're the one losing. Those are the situations where you need to apply grace. **Apply it liberally to all areas** and aspects of the marriage. Do not let any area remain untouched by this tool of grace.

The Marriage Manual

Hopefully you understand what I mean about grace after reading that paragraph. If you've felt the grace of God in your life, then you know how powerful and important grace is. If you haven't ever felt grace and its incredible liberating power, I'm not sure I can adequately explain it, but I'll give it a try.

Pretend you're a 10 year-old old kid who has grown up your entire life in an orphanage, raised by the staff who work at the orphanage. One day you go up to the staff and ask them about love. You've been hearing people talk about this word, and you thought you knew what it meant, but you're not sure, so you ask:

"Tell me what this kind of love feels like."

The staff go on to tell you things like:

Staff: It's that feeling when you really like something a lot.

You: Like ice cream?

Staff: Yes, but bigger and better. It's like that, but also that feeling you get when you care for someone a lot.

You: Like the staff here! I guess that means I love you guys! Is it like that?

Staff: Kind of, but there are different kinds of love.

You: There is more than one love?

Staff: Yeah, there are lots of different kinds. (Then the staff go into trying to explain the different types of love: agape, eros, philia, etc.)

You: But sometimes I get mad at the staff and yell. Does that mean I don't love them anymore?

Staff: No, you can love someone and be angry at them sometimes.

You: So love is a feeling that you have, but it's a different feeling depending on who you are loving—you love someone and can be angry with them, and you can love more than one person, and you can love them, but they might not love you?!

Staff: Yep, that's pretty much it!

My point with this story is to illustrate that it's tough to explain a feeling, and even harder to explain a feeling that you have never fully experienced. If in the above story you had grown up in a family where you were shown and felt loved, maybe even a had a crush on a peer, and someone asked you if you knew what love was you would say yes. It's the same with grace. You can kind of explain it, but if you haven't felt it, it's really hard to grasp.

The simple version of grace for the sake of marriage is this: Grace simply means there's going to be a time in your marriage where you're hurt and owed more from your spouse than he or she is able to give you, and you simply say, "We're good." Grace is the act of forgiving a debt that cannot be repaid.

Now, if your brain starts racing with all the ways this concept can be abused, you're missing the point of grace. It's so much bigger than that. If you've experienced grace, you know. This tool is essential—it needs to coat and cover the entire marriage. You cannot use too much grace. Grace is like the oil for the engine. It needs to cover all the moving parts. If you're struggling in your marriage and you want a healthy one, grace is a tool that is absolutely required. If you're newly married and haven't needed a lot of grace yet, you must be reading this book on your honeymoon, because trust me, you will need some grace soon.

If you don't have grace in your toolkit but you need it, there's some great news for you: Grace is free! The best way to experience grace is to ask Jesus for forgiveness for everything you have done wrong and will do wrong, and in return you get unconditional love. If you want grace, you might as well start at the top with some grace from Jesus!

Here is an example of grace in a marriage that may help illustrate how it can work and how it not only applies to great big issues such as affairs and deceptions in marriages, but also to everyday interactions.

DAVID AND VICTORIA.

David and Victoria came into counseling not having any major difficulties, just some challenges that they wanted to work on. They had been married for 12 years. They have three kids and both described their marriage as pretty good. We covered some normal challenges and arguments that most couples have and they were able to make some good progress that made things run even smoother. David and Victoria had one issue that although minor, they brought up to see if I could help them with. Often couples will want to tell their story and have me pick whose side is right. This felt like it was going to be one of those times.

David shared that he's frustrated with his wife because she will frequently set her alarm early in the morning. She will then proceed to hit snooze multiple times before she finally gets up. David becomes angry when this happens because he feels like this is disrespectful and preventable. David will frequently ask Victoria not to do this. Victoria will sometimes get frustrated when David asks her not to do this and will set her alarm for later. Victoria agreed with the majority of what David shared. She only wanted to add that she does try not to snooze the alarm and will do well with getting up when it first goes off for a period of time, but then she will go back to her old behavior. David shared that if Victoria were truly sorry, she would not keep doing the behavior. Victoria said that the fact that she tries and does well for a while shows that she is trying to be respectful, but she is just going to fail sometimes.

David and Victoria go on to share that they both have tried many different tactics to solve this problem. Sometimes David will get mad and yell at Victoria in the morning to just get up, sometimes Victoria will sleep in a different room to try to be considerate to David or even to punish him (they could never decide which it actually was.) David and Victoria did not want to end their evening or start their day in a negative manner. They then looked at me for a verdict on how this issue should be solved.

I told them the alarm clock issue might be something that may not be solved. It may be a circumstance where David needs to show grace to Victoria. David needs to realize that regardless of how he feels, his wife is trying and will not always meet his expectations. He has to decide how he wants to respond when she fails. He can yell and share how frustrated he is that she is so disrespectful, or her can accept that Victoria is going to snooze the alarm and kindly ask her to do better. That is grace. And remember, it's easier to show grace when it is experienced. Victoria reminded David (😊) that she also offers grace to him when he doesn't always put his dishes in the dishwasher.

Understanding that there will be times in your marriage when you will have to forgive and continue on is really difficult, but when you've been given this same gift of grace from God without deserving it, grace for your spouse becomes a lot easier to share. Having given grace to your spouse makes both the communication and the fighting go much smoother, just like oil makes a machine run better. Remembering that your goal is a healthy marriage and not to simply be right or prove your spouse wrong makes a big difference, too. Remember this old saying about marriage: Do you want to be right, or do you want to be married?!

Grace

— **NOTES** —

— NOTES —

— TOOL #5 —

COMMITMENT

The last tool you will need for a healthy marriage is commitment. You need to be committed to your marriage. A number of marriages will fail because the spouses are not all in. Be intentional with this. This is what is meant by the phrase "marriage is work." **You can't be kind of committed.**

Having the approach that no matter what happens, you are going to work at being the best spouse that you can be regardless of what the other person is doing, is the attitude you need to have a healthy marriage. This can be extremely hard if you've had some trouble in the past. One of the biggest stumbling blocks for couples who come into therapy is waiting too long to ask for help. Their commitment is waning. They have been hurt, but they're willing to give the marriage one last try if their partner is. The problem here

 YOU CAN'T KIND OF BE COMMITTED

is one spouse thinks he will give it one last try if his wife is willing to, and then they're both waiting for the other person to make the first move. They're not going to try to save the marriage until their spouse shows some interest in saving the marriage. Now we are in a stalemate, and each spouse is watching for something to happen, but neither one is committed to the process.

Each person is kind of "in," but with conditions. In this situation, both spouses say things like, "I will try when I see her doing something different," or, "When he starts helping me out around the house I will spend more time with him." This is not commitment.

You can also be committed to the wrong thing in marriage. Being committed to the fact that things will never get better and just settling is a commitment that has caused a number of marriages to remain stuck and miserable. Determining that things will always be like this is a dangerous thing to commit to, but be careful, this type of commitment will happen slowly over time. Eventually, you find yourself in a place that you never could have imagined. You realize you're okay with things that you never would have been okay with when you first got married.

HENRY AND MARGE.

Henry and Marge have been married for 30 years. They have two kids, ages 23 and 27. Their kids are out of the house, but both of the kids live in town and will visit Henry and Marge occasionally.

Henry and Marge initially went to counseling about 13 years ago. At that time Henry had an anger problem, and Marge was passive-aggressive and always complaining.

Here's an excerpt from a typical session where very little progress is made:

Therapist: Hey guys! How has your week been?

Marge: Fine.

Henry: Okay.

Therapist: *(Recognizing that those are two safe answers that really convey nothing other than that neither person wants to share anything of substance for fear that I as the therapist will want to talk about it. They're right. I'm going to push them to take some ownership of the session and their marriage because I've learned that they are more than happy to let me talk about ideas and things that couples can work on in a broad context.)* Well, what do you guys want to work on and talk about today? I haven't been part of your lives for the last week, so tell me where you got stuck or frustrated.

Marge: Well, you know, it was a typical week. I asked Henry what he wanted for supper, and he got angry and yelled at me, so I didn't say much.

Henry: I yelled at you because you insulted me! You told me that I never come home on time and I don't care about you!

Marge: I only said that it would be nice if you came home on time and let me know if you were going to be late!

The Marriage Manual

Therapist: So what are you guys really fighting about right now? *(Neither one of them wanted to solve anything, instead they kept making statements that they knew the other would respond to.)*

Marge: Well, I guess I would just like if he wouldn't yell at me.

Henry: I wouldn't yell if you would just be patient and not always judge me!

Therapist: *(Stopping them before they get started on the next round of finger-pointing about what they do or don't do.)* Okay great. Marge, are you willing to try and be a little more patient with Henry? Henry, are you ready to try and not resort to yelling so quickly?

Marge: I guess.

Henry: Okay.

Notice that both Henry and Marge gave uncommitted answers. We would go on to talk about other situations. I would even bring up some of their feelings in a bold manner because they never dared to do so. They would listen and sometimes agree, even shed some tears when I would articulate their feelings without them having to say them out loud, but when it came time to actually take a risk and do something different, neither Henry nor Marge ever ventured out to change their behavior. They felt safe with how things were. Not happy, but safe and predictable.

Marge would always complain about how bad her husband was, but she would stay safe by not working on anything in their marriage. If things got too close and personal for her, Marge would just start up a conversation about something Henry did that was not good. Henry would get angry but would call Marge out in a way that made sure he didn't have to do anything. He was comfortable to just sit back and let his wife complain. If things got too personal, Henry would bring up something that Marge did and that would take the focus off him.

Henry and Marge didn't make much progress in therapy because they kept blaming the other person, and neither one of them genuinely believed anything would change. They both agreed that they were miserable in the marriage but didn't think anything would be any different after counseling. So Henry and Marge dropped out of therapy. Recently, Marge has returned alone. I asked her how things were going. She said they are still the same. The only real difference is that they have stopped yelling and simply rarely talk to each other at all. She describes her and Henry as miserable, but comfortable. She returns, wondering if there is anything she can do to make things go a little better.

As we talked, it became clear that Marge is still in the same spot she was 13 years ago! She was looking for ways she could feel better without having to make too many changes or deal with Henry directly, but she also didn't want to leave him. Marge didn't want to change, instead she wanted to come in to therapy and tell me how bad things were, without any real intention of doing anything different in her marriage.

Henry and Marge are in a committed relationship. They are committed to each other. They will never leave each other. They will most likely spend the next 20 years together, rarely talking and occasionally getting angry, and that will be the extent of any real connection they share. This is not the kind of commitment you want. The impact that this has on children in the family is incredibly sad. Marge and Henry thought they were staying together for the kids, but this negative commitment has had a detrimental effect on their kids and how they view relationships.

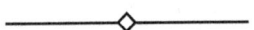

Not giving your spouse a chance is another form of not being committed to the relationship. Judging your spouse on all their past behaviors and assuming they will continue that pattern has doomed many marriages.

I will often explain a communication idea about the importance of sharing feelings with your spouse to couples in my therapy office. I will then hear a story from one of the spouses and ask him if he told his wife his feelings.

"Why would I tell her that?" the husband asks me. "She will just say I'm whiny and needy. She always does that."

He may even be right that his wife always does that, but I want him to see that she USED to do that. He did not even give her the chance to change or do things differently, even when they were both sitting in therapy. Even if his spouse does things the old way now, we can talk to her about her commitment level and her willingness to try and do things differently, but we can't get on her if she never even had the chance to grow and change.

Commitment involves you, and you alone. You have to decide how much you want to give to the marriage. How much do you want to change? How much do you want to grow? If you don't have this willingness to grow and change, your marriage will not be healthy. Focus on being the spouse you want to be regardless of what is going on around you.

JACK AND DIANNE.

Jack and Dianne had been married for two years. This was the second marriage for both of them. Their previous spouses both cheated on them and they eventually each left. Jack and Dianne both came into their current relationship with some fears about faithfulness and the same pattern repeating itself. Jack had two kids from his first marriage, and Dianne had three. They also had a baby together that was two months old.

Jake and Dianne came in to therapy because Dianne felt like the marriage was in trouble. Dianne recently caught Jack texting a female acquaintance. Their texting conversations weren't sexual, but Jack acknowledged that he knew his wife would be mad. Dianne shared that this was why she thinks the marriage is not going to work. Jack told me that he stopped texting the female acquaintance five months ago, and he hasn't done anything since. Dianne said she feels like it's just a matter of time before something like this happens again.

Jack talked about how earlier in their relationship Dianne had also had some inappropriate contact with another guy that was more sexual in nature, but Jack moved on. Dianne said that incident happened because Jack was always working and didn't give her enough time and attention. Jack argued that he was working so much because she wanted to stay home and not work. Dianne then shared that Jack expected her to do everything.

This arguing went around and around. Everything that one spouse would say, the other spouse had an answer for, and that answer usually involved how the other spouse failed. This couple was amazingly good at always pointing out why things were bad and how it started with the other person. Therapy would go in circles with me trying to stop the cycle of blame and get them to start working on the marriage. Every time I would bring up a way to do something different, Jack and Dianne would actually take turns telling me why that idea would not work because their spouse wouldn't change. They were so scared of getting hurt again that it was much safer to stay committed to the current situation than work on anything. **Commitment is about being committed to your spouse's potential for what they can become, not what they have always done.**

I finally challenged Jack and Dianne to stop pointing out what their spouse was doing because it tended to be negative. I ended up giving them each an assignment to do regardless of what their spouse was doing. They were not allowed to provide me with a report on each other! I did this to try and get them out of the routine of waiting to see if their spouse was going to take the first step.

FOCUS ON BEING A GOOD SPOUSE, NOT BEING GOOD TO YOUR SPOUSE

Jack and Dianne both kept waiting for the other person to get started. The goal with commitment is to **focus on being a good spouse, not being good to your spouse.** You can be the man/woman you want to be without any input from your spouse. Jack and Dianne were also given the challenge to not say anything at all if you can't say something nice so they couldn't sabotage each other. They were only allowed to compliment each other on what they noticed, nothing else. They were not even allowed to comment on how well their spouse was doing their homework, only what they liked.

It took a long time to break Jack and Dianne's habit of bringing up old behaviors, but they gradually began to see the commitment and follow-through in one another, and not simply see all the old behaviors they assumed would not change. You need to be committed to the process—you don't need your spouse to be committed to changing before you join in.

— NOTES —

— OPTIONAL EQUIPMENT/EXTRAS —

YOUR SPOUSE

Hopefully you have a marriage with extra features, i.e., a spouse that also wants to have a healthy marriage along with you. Up until now, all the tools that you have needed for a healthy marriage are individual. If you can include your spouse in your toolkit and they are willing to work on doing things differently, it will significantly increase the benefits and features of your marriage. Can you get your spouse on board? Have you asked them?

Most of the time in my experience, it's the man who is against counseling. This makes sense because men are typically reluctant to ask for help and would just as soon tough it out. Interestingly, men are also less likely to read instruction manuals! (Hopefully they will read this one!) Often the man will come into my office and I will ask him why he is here, and he says, "My wife made me come here today." I will act surprised and say something like, "Really! How did she do that?! She doesn't look that strong. Is she able to carry you?"

He responds with, "No, but she said if I don't come, she will leave me." I reframe what he is saying into a more positive approach that will help in counseling.

"Oh, so you're here today because you don't want your wife to leave? That is an awesome reason to come in today!" Helping him see that he doesn't only have a choice to make, but also that he is choosing to work on his marriage is something I want the man and his spouse to see.

Men tend to not want to come in for counseling for a variety of reasons. They may be afraid that they are going to be told what to do. Some are embarrassed by their poor behaviors. Some are afraid that all we will do is talk about their past. Some are afraid of feelings and worried that they will become a soft, blubbering guy. There are a number of plausible reasons, so if you're trying to get your spouse to come to therapy and have not been successful, have you used the communication tool to find out why your spouse is reluctant to go to therapy?

Knowing what your spouse is afraid of can help you hear and solve the problem of getting them to come to therapy. Do you understand what he's saying when you're hearing his answers, or are you just telling him that he's dumb and to get over it? How have you asked him to go to therapy? When did you ask him to go to therapy? Frequently this discussion is held in the middle of a fight! Remember your fighting lessons—it's not a good idea to share feelings while you're angry. If the only time a couple talks about marriage counseling is when they're in the middle of a fight and everyone is upset and yelling, most of the time getting to therapy is not going to work. How about you have that conversation after things are calmed down?

How you frame going to counseling is important as well. Yelling, "You're so mean and hurtful and you don't understand

and we need to go to counseling so you can figure out how to treat me better!" is usually a proposition that a man is not going to jump on too quickly. Sharing that same sentiment in a different manner when things are calm and you have not had a fight is an entirely different story. Asking your husband to go to counseling so you can learn how to communicate better is helpful. How about even saying, "I'm having trouble understanding what you need and what you're always trying to tell me. Can we go to counseling together so I can figure out what you are trying to say to me, because I'm not getting it?" That way of saying things is way more likely to get him to counseling. If none of those tactics work, you can always do the old, "If you don't go, I'm going to leave." Just be careful, ultimatums are dangerous in marriage.

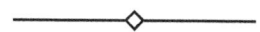

SUCCESS!

You have now completed and assembled a healthy marriage! Congratulations. You have all the tools you need. A word of caution: do not put these tools away, you will need them frequently. Ideally, on a daily basis.

It's important to remember why you've purchased this marriage and why you're using the tools in this manual. You wanted a healthy marriage. It will be work. Why did you want a healthy marriage? It's important to review and spend some time thinking about why you're doing all this work. Typically it's because it feels awesome to be loved and valued. It also feels awesome to make someone else feel loved a valued. Being in a healthy marriage will make so many areas of your life feel better and smoother. If you feel loved, safe, and valued, how do you think that will impact your kids, your job, your friends? If you have the feeling that no matter what you have someone in your corner at all times, you will take risks, challenge yourself, grow, and be even more satisfied in this world. When you feel this way, it will seem like it's you and your spouse together against the world. Bring it on! When it's just you against the world, it's a much lonelier and scarier place—having someone in your corner with you changes your perspective immensely.

You are now ready to use your healthy marriage—enjoy it, have fun, and good luck!

You may be thinking, *Wait! What?? That's it?! It can't be!*

Yep, it actually is. Just remember, these tools need to be used daily for a healthy marriage. If you feel like you don't have a healthy marriage at this point, just like any other manual, I have included a troubleshooting guide. Just like that new TV you bought comes with a troubleshooting guide, saying things like, "If your TV doesn't turn on, check if it's plugged in. Check to see if the power cord is connected to the television." This marriage manual will also ask if you've done this or checked that. Sometimes manuals will say things like, "Your fuse will need to be replaced." The best and easiest fix—have you updated the software?

Have you updated your marriage software? Well, you're in luck, this marriage manual also comes with a troubleshooting guide and software update.

Your Spouse

— **NOTES** —

—PART 2—
TROUBLESHOOTING GUIDE

Here are some things to look for if your marriage is currently not functioning correctly. I have organized this troubleshooting guide under various topics that can cause your marriage not to work properly. Feel free to read them all, or to simply read the ones that apply to your situation. Remember to save this manual and refer back to it as needed.

— NOTES —

— TROUBLESHOOTING GUIDE —

TIME

One trouble spot that can happen in a marriage is getting too busy to have time to use the marriage tools effectively. If you're not around to communicate with your spouse, that connection gets lost. You can survive brief periods of time when you're not connecting, but if this separation lasts too long, problems will develop.

If you don't take time to connect, you and your spouse will begin to feel like roommates. You are both in the same house doing your thing, but there is no togetherness. You are both accomplishing the things that need to happen in a day, but you tend to go through the motions. When busy couples do finally have some time to connect, they spend that time in the same house but not together. If you're so busy and tired from your day, couples often just veg out on the couch but don't really connect. Often your marriage is put at the bottom of this pile of things to spend time on, and then we wonder why we just feel like roommates.

Feeling like roommates is a really bad spot to be in when you are actually more than roommates. It's at this stage that

I will often hear one spouse say that they think they no longer love their spouse anymore, or they're just not "in love." If the other spouse is present in the room when this is said, they're often upset, hurt, and worried. I understand that this is a hard thing to hear, but I'm not usually worried about it as a therapist. I know the reason this couple is not in love is simply because they have lost that connection, and it's often due to lack of time spent together.

FEELING LIKE ROOMMATES IS A REALLY BAD SPOT WHEN YOU ARE ACTUALLY MORE THAN ROOMMATES

I can illustrate this to the couple by asking the wife a hypothetical question. I say, "Look out the window and imagine that a nice guy walked by, and I asked you, 'do you want to go home with him?'"

What does she usually say back? **"No, I don't even know him!"** Why is she not interested in that person? She doesn't know him. You can have the same problem with your spouse. Why do you not feel in love with him? You don't know him. If you take the time to understand your spouse, you will want to spend more time with him and feel connected.

You can solve this time problem by looking at the things in your life that are taking time away from your spouse. It can be a variety of things: kids' hobbies, Netflix, being on your phone, work—there can be a multitude of reasons. Being lazy and expecting your spouse to make all the effort to connect with you can cause the time problem to be even bigger than it needs to be. Are you working at finding time to be with your spouse, or are you only waiting for your spouse to come to you? Are you so busy at work that either you are never home or when you are home, you have no energy or time to give to your spouse?

One of the biggest dangers in a marriage is technology and social media. Are you spending so much time on your phone or iPad that you're not only not talking to your spouse, but you're also filling your head with a photoshopped world that you wish you could belong to instead of your own? Are you bingeing Netflix shows, even if it's with your spouse, and never communicating? When I first started marriage counseling, there was a big push to make sure you had TVs out of your bedroom because couples would watch the TV instead of talking. Unfortunately, phones are usually right next to the nightstand now, and there are two of them in the room. We will often make sure our kids don't have their phones in their bedrooms, but we're not as diligent with ourselves. Make a plan or goal for how long you can be on your phone before bed. **Many marriage problems begin in the quiet scrolling of two people in a bed together, not talking.**

Make time for your marriage and use the tools, and you will see benefits pretty quickly. Remember the communication technique of creating the right environment. If you can carve out 30 minutes for you and your spouse to sit on the couch and talk about how you're doing, you will be amazed by how quickly loving feelings come back.

— NOTES —

— TROUBLESHOOTING GUIDE —

CHILDREN

Children can also be a reason your marriage is not healthy. This is similar to time, but often this is a decision that both you and your spouse are making. According to statistics and surveys, **marital satisfaction is often at its lowest when children are in the house**[4].

That is a scary statistic because when you have children in the house is often the longest chunk of time that you're married. Hopefully couples have put in the work to communicate and fight in a healthy manner, because when kids come along, they are going to have to be much more efficient at those things. Often spouses will be great moms and dads, but lousy wives and husbands. Meaning, you put all your effort into being a dad and not much effort into being a husband.

Kids take a lot of time and effort. Complicating matters, we usually make this sacrifice wholeheartedly. If I tell you that your spouse only has a limited amount of time and energy to

---

[4] VanLaningam J, Johnson DR, Amato Pr. "Marital Happiness, Marital Duration, and the U-Shaped Curve: Evidence from a Five-Wave Panel Study," Social Forces, 2001: 79:1313-1341.

give today, do you want it to go to your kids or to you? Most of us would willingly say give it to our kids, you will wait. That's very noble and loving but make that sacrifice all the time and now you're not feeling connected to your spouse.

Finding ways to balance your marriage and your kids is extremely important. This is especially true when you have an infant. Babies require so much time and attention that you usually barely have anything left for yourself, let alone for your spouse. When you're running on empty and looking for your spouse to fill you up and they're also empty, that can be a recipe for disaster.

There have been a number of studies done that show children negatively impact satisfaction in your marital relationship. Kids can certainly bring joy and happiness to your lives and eventually add to your marital bliss, but you need to get through a significant part of the parenting challenges before you and your spouse feel like you have a handle on things.

Having kids at home is going to be one of the biggest time cycles in your marriage, so what can you do to make that time a healthy season for you and your spouse? Finding a routine and making time for your marriage is key. It probably won't be balanced equally between parenting and being a good spouse, but you need to carve out time for your marriage. That can mean finding a babysitter and having a date night out, or even something more realistic like having a "date night" where once or twice a week after the kids are in bed you take 30 minutes to sit on the couch and talk. Even this kind of date can do wonders for your marriage. Make sure that when you're talking, the conversation is focused on your relationship, not on your jobs or the kids. You will be tired when you're having these conversations, but having this routine will keep the connection to your spouse healthy.

Remember, when you have children you have to seek out moments to actively connect—these moments will rarely just present themselves. But if you're looking for them, you can find them. Even 45 minutes while you're waiting for your child's practice to be done, or 30 minutes while they're in piano lessons can be turned into times to connect. Sometimes running these errands, even though it will only take one of you to do the task, will give you some time together to connect.

— NOTES —

— TROUBLESHOOTING GUIDE —

NO HELP

No help is a problem where your marriage has developed some bad habits. This usually starts with poor communication. Couples who do not communicate about the expectations of roles and jobs in marriage still have those roles and responsibilities, and they tend to evolve over time. The problem with not communicating about roles and responsibilities in marriage is that the jobs to be done don't grow equally. This is especially true if you have a spouse who is super efficient and organized and a spouse who tends to be more relaxed and laid back.

Think about all the roles you and your spouse have in marriage. In premarital counseling, I will often encourage couples to talk about these things and come to some kind of agreement on who is going to do what in the marriage. These agreements can change and switch around, but it's often helpful if they are talked about. Here's an example: in your marriage, who cleans the house or apartment? How did you decide this? Did you sit down and talk about who will clean the bathrooms, who will vacuum the floors, dust, etc., or did it just happen? Sometimes whoever does the job first just starts doing it, and it's never really discussed.

The Marriage Manual

Like most not-super-fun-jobs like cleaning, as soon as it's not getting done, a fight erupts. Who goes grocery shopping in your marriage? Why doesn't the other spouse do it? What does the other spouse do instead of grocery shopping? If you don't know these answers, you will have some resentment about the things you're doing in the marriage. If the answer is simply, "I go grocery shopping because my spouse would not know how to do it, so I just do it," you will definitely have the feeling that he/she never helps you. As soon as you have that conversation about who is doing the grocery shopping and why, and you know that you don't have to do the oil changes in the car, things start to feel better.

There are also more fun tasks in a marriage that couples need to talk about. How often do you guys eat dinner together? Every night? Only when you both happen to be home at supper time? How often will you guys go to bed together at the same time? Remember, people's numbers don't match, so often one person will want to go to bed early while the other stays up late. Usually, couples don't talk about these things and are left feeling all alone or like there is no help for them. Have you guys sat down and talked about your expectations for marriage in terms of going to bed together, or do you simply yell, "When are you coming to bed?!"

Frequently when a spouse is feeling all alone, they have not adequately shared their expectations for the roles and jobs in a marriage. They have just done the jobs themself because someone needs to do them. The other spouse just assumes the one who usually does them will get things done because they typically do, and the relationship gradually grows apart. If you're feeling alone and think you are the only one working in the marriage, you may be right. Have the conversation with your spouse—not about what they are not doing, but about what the roles and jobs are and who's doing what. Your spouse may see how imbalanced things are and that the marriage doesn't look like a partnership, and or you may see how many jobs your spouse is doing that you were unaware of and you will not feel like you're not getting any help.

Here is a list of everyday things that are usually not talked about but need to be if you feel like you have no help in your marriage:

1. Who cleans the house?
2. Who mows the lawn?
3. Who goes grocery shopping?
4. Who put the kids to bed?
5. Who helps with homework?
6. Who takes the kids to practice?
7. Who pays the bills?
8. Who does the laundry?
9. Who changes the oil in the cars?
10. Who shovels the snow?
11. How often do you eat meals together?
12. How often do you go to bed together?
13. How often do you want to have sex?
14. How often do you want to go out?

There may be many other roles and jobs that you will become aware of once you start communicating about these things. Hopefully you can come to an agreement where you don't feel like you're left to do all the marriage jobs by yourself.

— NOTES —

— TROUBLESHOOTING GUIDE —

IN-LAWS/PARENTS

In-laws can be a potential challenge to a healthy marriage. Instead of talking about and focusing on all the challenging things that in-laws and parents can do to impact a marriage, let's focus on the positives. First, a healthy thing to do is remember that all marriages need boundaries. It can sometimes be challenging for parents to stop parenting. Often parents have not met much resistance to their parenting until their child gets married and the other spouse starts to set some boundaries. This is a precarious time. Boundaries need to be placed in a new marriage. Don't get lazy. **Lazy people set boundaries for their in-laws, not their own parents.** It's much easier to complain about your spouse's parents and point out how they do things differently and how they're not helpful when they're so involved in your marriage. It's way harder to identify those things in your own parents.

Have you ever noticed that your spouse can express all kinds of frustrations about their own parents, but when you do the same thing the roles get switched, and then your spouse is defending them? Your spouse can say that he is frustrated because his parents never listen and talk right over him, but

 LAZY PEOPLE SET BOUNDARIES FOR THEIR IN LAWS NOT THEIR OWN PARENTS.

as soon as you say his family sometimes doesn't listen when you're talking, your spouse says, "Oh, that's just my parents, they always do that, they just get excited and like to talk." It's for that reason that when you're talking about in-laws and parents, you need to be really good with your communication skills. Frequently the conversation will be challenging and not always feel fair.

There are many couples where one spouse talks to their parents frequently—some even talk every day. This is dangerous. A general guideline for dealing with your parents and in-laws is that you should not be communicating with them more than you are with your own spouse. If you are talking to a parent every day that means you are talking to your spouse even more every day.

Along with this is being aware of what you're sharing with your parents or in-laws. What topics are off-limits, what can and can't you say to your in-laws? There are some topics that if you want to make sure you have a healthy marriage, you need to stay away from. Two topics that are most often talked about when they shouldn't be are money and fighting. When you and your spouse are in a fight, the last thing you want to do is tell your parents or your in-laws about the fight. Why? Because they're your parents. Your parents will always take your side. It's what parents should do. Recall what you learned about fighting earlier. Fighting is not about sides. Your goal is not to get more people on your side, but to be able to share your side. When you communicate with your parents that you're fighting, they will take your side and reinforce the whole your side versus my side issue, which is not something you want to do. Involving parents just makes for more work, after you have solved the problem with your spouse, then you have to solve it with your parents or in-laws. Don't make more work for yourself.

Involving your parents in your financial struggles is also a recipe for disaster. It has long been said that you don't lend money to friends because it will ruin a friendship. It will also destroy a relationship if you involve borrowing money from parents or in-laws. There are a hundred ways this can go wrong, and if it goes right, it still feels awkward and uncomfortable. Borrowing money from your parents or in-laws not only creates an imbalance between you and your parents or in-laws, but it also creates an imbalance between you and your spouse. You will rarely feel the pressure of owing money equally. Even if you are actively paying off whatever loan you have, typically you have not communicated with your parents or spouse what the repayment looks like. It just ends up hanging over your heads … unequally. An imbalance is never healthy in a marriage.

— NOTES —

— TROUBLESHOOTING GUIDE —

MONEY

Money is one of the "big three" when it comes to troubleshooting. The big three are the three topics couples will need to deal with for the duration of their marriage. That is a nice way of saying that there are three topics that all couples will fight/disagree/need to resolve for their whole marriage. Religion, sex, and money are the big three. That is because these things are ever-changing and evolving, so not only will your numbers not match, they will keep changing!

Money is important. Agreement on what to do with it is essential! Money is the second biggest area where couples struggle in marriage. There are so many challenges that come with money because it's not simply about numbers—emotions and feelings are attached to money as well.

If you're having a lot of challenges with your spouse over money, it may be helpful to start at the beginning and, as always, start with yourself, not your spouse. Take some time to reflect on what it was like for you financially growing up. A number of your impressions about money will be formed during this time. What was the financial situation of your family like growing up? Did they have money? Did they value it? Did they spend it wisely, or blow it? Was money a source of arguments for your parents? Who was in charge of the money, one spouse or equally? Who paid the bills? Did your parents frequently tell you, "We don't have any money for that," or did they make sure you always had everything you needed? Did you have an allowance? How did you get the money? Did you have any special rules about how you could spend it?

The answers to all those questions will begin to highlight your view and relationship with money. You need to have a good understanding of this before you even go and talk with your spouse about money. You need to be aware of your personality and views about money while you're talking to your spouse. Next, obviously, you need to find out your spouse's perspective on money. You may have an idea, but make sure you get his or her own input on the subject.

Now that you have your perspective about money and your spouse's, you can begin to move forward to figure out what your family, you, and your spouse's approach to money is going to be. There are a number of things that I do in premarital counseling that, if you have not done, would be beneficial to talk about.

First, how much money do you need to have in your savings account to feel safe? Remember, as you talk about these things, your answers aren't going to be based on logic, but on feelings. Your feelings will be different from your spouse's, but that doesn't mean those feelings are wrong. Remember, your numbers won't match!

You identify that you feel comfortable with $1,000 dollars in your savings account and then you will feel safe. Let's say your spouse comes up with $10,000 dollars to feel safe—she wants to have enough to pay her bills for a couple of months. Now pretend (unfortunately, most couples don't have to pretend because they have never communicated deeply about money) you don't know this about your spouse, and you have $5,000 dollars in your saving account. How are you feeling? Probably great! You have the view that you as a couple are doing awesome! We have $4,000 extra dollars that we can spend! You tell your spouse that you guys need to go on vacation and have some fun! But your spouse says, "No, we don't have the money." Now the fight begins, and it ends with you thinking your spouse is a penny pincher and she thinking that you're stupid with money and blow it all the time.

Now, go back and think about how your spouse feels when she has $5,000 in the savings account. She is thinking you are halfway to the goal, and you come along and want to spend some money. That is why she tells you no, we can't go, because she feels like you guys don't have enough money. Now, if you communicate and learn this about each other and practice what you have learned, you can come to a compromise about how much money you guys together have picked to have in your savings account. It should be some nice compromise around $5,000. This allows you as a couple to work together and not feel like your spouse is sabotaging things.

Second, who is going to be in charge of paying the bills? In the old days, this question was, who is going to write out the checks when they come in? Now this is more about who is going to oversee the automatic withdrawals and make sure

The Marriage Manual

IF YOU ARE THE ONE IN CHARGE OF PAYING THE BILLS YOU ARE NOT THE ONE IN CHARGE OF THE MONEY.

everything is doing what it's supposed to be doing. Usually in couples there is one person who tends to be more organized and on top of things. There is usually someone who is gifted at managing numbers and staying accountable. Frequently that person is the one who ends up doing this job.

Now, here comes the tricky part: **If you are the one in charge of paying the bills, you are not the one in charge of the money.** Those are two different things that often get mixed up. Too often the person in charge of writing the checks and paying the bills takes on too much responsibility, and the other spouse becomes lazy and allows the other person to take control. This works okay when things are going smoothly, but when life happens or bumps in the road occur and now you don't have enough money to pay the bills, the person managing the bills feels responsible. They are stuck, so they will typically go to their spouse and say they don't have enough money. If you are the spouse who has not been writing the bills, what do you say? "Where did all the money go?" There is no way to ask that question without starting a fight. Now, in that spouse's defense, that is an excellent question. He has not been paying attention, he does not know what is going on and is asking you to update him and let him know where all the money went. Unfortunately, your spouse is answering that question while already feeling responsible for somehow failing, and it becomes a mess.

When you guys decide who the person in charge of paying the bills is, I want you both to have the view that the person paying the bills is only the secretary. Meaning that person is only doing what has been decided on by the boss. The person who is in charge of the budget is the boss. And who is the boss? Both of you! In a healthy marriage, you both together set the budget, and when the budged does not work, you both figure it out. The person paying the bills is just following through with what the two of you decided. There are many ways of doing this—having budget meetings and planning for how you guys want to spend money would be helpful. Remember, if you're the bill payer, you are not responsible when there are problems. You are not in charge of solving those issues. If you're not the bill payer, you are not off the hook. Yes, you have to help set the budget, but that is not your only job. You need to be engaged in the process.

You should never be surprised when your spouse comes to you and says you guys have a money issue. You should be able to see that coming. One way my wife and I did this when we were first married was by playing a game to make sure I was doing my part. My wife was the bill payer (she's a math teacher, good with numbers, and organized), so she would periodically ask me how much money we had in the checking account. I had to get within $50 of the actual amount (we didn't have much money starting out). My wife could usually get within the penny because she was paying attention, balancing, and watching the account closely. If I didn't periodically take the time to check the checkbook, I would miss things, and that clearly meant I was not working on keeping our budget as much as she was.

This practice helped me stay on top of our finances, so when she would come to me and say we were short on money, I was able to say I saw that coming. I would ask her, "What do you think we should do?" instead of, "Where did it all go?" This game would be way easier in the age of technology. I would have been able to just pull it up on my phone! If you're not the one paying the bills, you should at least be checking your accounts periodically and seeing how you are doing. When you pull up your account are you relieved? Scared? Do you share those feeling with your spouse?

One last thing with bank accounts. I will frequently get asked if it's better to have one account where everything goes or if you should each have a separate account and then one joint one? It doesn't matter how many bank accounts you have. This is not a reflection on the strength of your marriage. You need to remember one thing: No matter how many accounts you have or where your money is located, it is still **our money.** As long as you approach your conversations about money from the perspective that it is ours and not mine and hers, you will be okay. When you start to say things like, "That is my money" or, "I need some of your money," you're in trouble. The money is ours. When it's viewed as ours, it does not matter where the money is located. When money is considered to be our money, that means you each have an equal vote in where it goes. This is true regardless of who makes more money. Whether you're a doctor, lawyer, or stay-at-home mom, each of you has an equal vote on budgeting. You don't get more of a say because you make more. In a healthy marriage, it is an equal partnership.

The third big question that I ask couples about money is this: how much money can you spend without asking your spouse? You need to figure that out. Hopefully if you've worked on a budget, you will have talked about this as it's necessary information. You don't want to be standing in line a McDonald's and calling your wife to ask her if you can super-size the No. 4 meal! You also probably shouldn't walk in the house with a new 75-inch flat-screen TV without talking to her first!

Now, most couples will answer the question of how much you can spend without asking your spouse with, "it depends on what it is." Which is true and a good place to start. You probably don't have to ask about some things, but others you do. Who decides what is essential and what is not? This is an issue that will come up frequently in marriage. Who decides what is important to spend money on? Guess what, do you think you and your spouse will agree on the important things to spend money on? Figuring this out will eliminate a lot of arguments. You will not be able to stop every argument about money, but there is a way to reduce these arguments and solve a number of them. What is a more crucial monetary expense in marriage, makeup or hunting gear? A fun pair of wedge sandals or sporting event tickets? Lunch with some girlfriends or some beers with the guys? A shopping trip to the mall or a fishing trip to the lake? Getting your nails done or a new sports jersey? New couch or new four-wheeler? There are thousands of these dilemmas, and they are the ones that most couples end up fighting about. If you can find a way to eliminate as many

The Marriage Manual

of them as possible, that's ideal. Here's one way that my wife and I handle these types of questions:

I love drinking pop. I almost always have a pop on my desk that I'm drinking. When we were first married, I would come in the house drinking a pop that I bought at the gas station. When I walked in the door drinking it, my wife would say, "Why did you buy that pop? Why did you not take one from home? That would be cheaper. Why did you not buy a six-pack at the grocery store? That would be cheaper." She was right, of course. It would be cheaper to wait until I got home or to buy some pops from the grocery store. What she did not understand was that I liked to get out of the office and drive around and run to the gas station to buy a pop. I'm not thinking about the cheapest way to buy a pop—I'm looking at it from an enjoyable experience perspective.

We needed to figure out how to solve this fight. Neither one of us wanted to deal with the issue over and over again. Something needed to be done—the solution. Make an agreement or, in biblical terms, a covenant. We worked on our budget and looked at not what our gas station pop budget could be for the month, but on what we could each spend or, in my case, blow every month. Some couples call this an allowance or spending money. It doesn't matter what you call it, it matters that you respect the agreement. We set up an amount in our budget that we could each spend on whatever we wanted.

I spent my allowance mostly on pop, candy, and other crap. My wife, of course, spent hers on much wiser things! ☺ We did, however, solve the problem. Now when I walked into the house drinking a pop, she simply said, "how was your day?"

When she walked in with something that looked expensive, meaning more than what our monthly spending limit was, I would ask her, "how did you buy that?" She would always reply, "Oh, it's my spending money. I've just been saving it up for a while!"

Finding a solution for what you think it's important to spend money on and how to reduce what you think are the "dumb things" your spouse is spending money on is something that couples need to solve if they want to reduce the number of marital arguments over money. Imagine how our marriage strengthens over time when both of us continue to follow the marital covenant or agreement we made. When my wife sees me walking into the house without a pop, she knows that I have probably spent my money for the month. Think about how safe she feels, knowing that yes, I blow money on dumb things, but I take our agreement seriously. When we both follow this and realize that we are both committed to being financially healthy regardless of what we want to spend money on, it makes future discussions on more significant topics with money much more manageable. When we are both able to know that we have been working together and honoring commitments with pops and manicures, we will certainly know that we can do that same thing with things like cars and mortgages.

The troubleshooting practice for money that you will want to make sure you do is have some goals. You should have a budget first. Then you should know why you have X amount in each category. Why are you not paying for cable? Why are you bringing your lunch from home instead of going out? Simply saving money is too broad and not a very clear goal.

You need to know why you are sacrificing, and you need to see the progress that you are making for your sacrifice. Make it clear to both of you why you're doing what you're doing. Can you visibly see where the money that you are saving is going? Have the goal of saving money for a vacation or adding an extra amount to your car payment. When you have a goal, know what it is. If you know you are not the only one working on that goal, it tends to get achieved faster. When you know your spouse is not sabotaging you or spending money as quickly as you're saving it, you will start to make some headway. Nothing is worse than making a sacrifice for your family monetarily only to come home and see your spouse has just bought something that you think is frivolous. Once you are both on the same page with the same goals, it's a huge relief and actually a marriage builder.

— NOTES —

— NOTES —

— TROUBLESHOOTING GUIDE —

BIG LIFE CHANGES

A potential trouble spot that all marriages will face at one point or another is big life changes. These are things that a marriage may or may not have planned for but are happening to the marriage and will change how the marriage functions and operates. These changes are not all bad.

When you add a child into your marriage, it can cause some major stress. Studies have revealed that the second-most stressful time in a marriage is when you add the first child to the marriage (the first is usually the second year of marriage, because that's when they honeymoon is over and things get real)[5].

There are a lot of reasons for this first child being so stressful. Typically a couple has just settled into their routine, and it has begun to run smoothly. They have communicated about the goals and expectations of marriage. Hopefully, they have learned how to live with each other without too much stress, and once everything is running smoothly,

---

[5] Aaron A, Norman C, Aaron E, Lewandowski G. "Shared Participation in Self-Expanding Activities," *Understanding Marriage: Developments in the Study of Couple Interaction.* New York: Cambridge University Press; 2002. Pp. 177-194.

YOUR SPOUSE MAY NOT SHARE VERY WELL

along comes a baby that changes every aspect of your life, including your marriage. Now all of a sudden you have to share your time and love with another person. **Your spouse may not share very well** and expect the same amount of time and attention they were getting from you before the baby. You will both be putting a lot of energy into a baby who needs constant care and attention. You will be empty and need to be filled up.

Before the baby, who filled you up and met your needs? Hopefully your spouse, but now you will be looking to your spouse to meet your needs, but they are empty and looking to you to meet theirs. Two empty people looking to take care of each other usually do not go well together. Finding out how to adjust and move forward from this big life change will take patience and communication. Using the same skills that you did the first time around when learning to adapt to being married will help you now. Learning to ask for help and make your needs known in a manner that does not make your spouse feel like they are failing is wise. Carving out brief periods to spend time together and using some support systems around you would also be good. It's amazing how much just a couple of hours without your child can help your marriage stabilize. Everything takes a little longer when you have a baby, even healthy communication in marriage.

Moving can also be a significant life change. When a family moves, there can be a lot of reasons why. Are you moving away from family or towards family? Losing a reliable babysitter and being in a different city can impact your marriage more than you may initially realize. Finding someone you can trust in a new city will need to be a priority. If you're moving towards family, learning and setting new boundaries will have to occur. Having family nearby can be helpful, but it also requires setting some boundaries and expectations, which typically are hard to do for some people. Keeping family out of a marriage is needed if you want to keep your marriage healthy.

Losing a job, getting fired, declaring bankruptcy, or getting laid off can add significant stress to a marriage. These things are rarely planned and will force a couple to communicate. If you have not been communicating well before, this lack of communication will make handling life changes that much more difficult. Unexpected challenges will push you and your spouse to make some choices that you may not want to make. Being on the same page together will make these choices a little less stressful. Remembering that you are trying to solve the problem, not change the person—meaning, don't make it personal—will make the stress a little more bearable. Being angry at your spouse because they got laid off may make you feel like you are doing something, but it does not solve the issue of how are going to proceed.

Another significant life change that can affect your marriage are health issues. These changes can impact your marriage much like having a child can. It may be a broken leg that you have which means your spouse is now taking on more responsibilities around the house. This may be only temporary, but it can cause extra stress and frustration on both spouses. What if the health issue is bigger or even permanent? Adjusting to a spouse who has a chronic illness or has changed as a result of an accident, stroke, or heart attack requires major adjustment and communication with each other. "For better or worse" takes on a whole new meaning when it actually is worse.

Communicating the challenges you are facing with your spouse, whether you have a chronic illness or are taking care of someone who has a chronic illness is an ongoing process. You will need to talk about things over and over. Don't avoid the subject or the problematic feelings. Often neither spouse wants to talk about the injury or illness for fear of how it will make the other spouse feel. It's dumb not to talk about something that you both feel and know exists. Take the plunge. Do the hard work. It will be worth it even if there are no easy answers, knowing that you are not left to feel these things by yourself can be very empowering.

Big Life Changes

— NOTES —

— NOTES —

— TROUBLESHOOTING GUIDE —

SEX

Of all the trouble spots in marriage, this is the one that I'm guessing everyone will probably be reading first before all the others. Sex is actually a good barometer of how your marriage is doing. Typically, you can't have a bad marriage but have a great sex life, and you can't have a great marriage and a lousy sex life. If your marriage is going well, your sex life should be going well. If you're struggling in your marriage, your sex life will be one of the first areas that will get your attention that things are not going well. Do not ignore this part of your marriage or think that it will just get better on its own.

When addressing sex problems, just like everything in all instruction manuals, go back to the beginning. Just like when your TV doesn't work, the first line of the instructions is to make sure it's plugged in! It's the same thing here, meaning, go back to Tool #1: You! Know yourself.

What was your previous experience with sex like? I will always ask premarital couples where they learned about sex. Most of the time I will get sheepish looks from them here.

Take some time and ask yourself, where did you learn about sex? Did your parents sit you down and give you "the talk"? Did you get the biology of how sex works from your health class? Did your friends tell you how it works? Did you learn about it from magazines, TV, movies, or the internet?

Is there any other subject that is so important to people but that they know so little about other than sex? Think about it for a second, do you believe everything you see in magazines, TV, and the internet? Crazy. If you were lucky enough to have your parents talk to you, what did they say? Did they teach you that sex was just for making children? Did they teach you sex was something that you just don't talk about? Did they teach you sex was bad? Most parents when talking to their children, if they talk to them at all, usually come with the perspective that you don't talk about sex and you don't have it until after you are married. Great! You're now married! Did they come back and give you the rest of the story now? Were you ever taught that sex is needed, healthy, good, fun, and even awesome? I'm hoping that after examining your views on sex you can see that you have a problem.

If you were raised like most people, you were taught very little in terms of information about sex that will be helpful in a loving relationship. Sex is powerful, which is why it is used to sell, motivate, and get your attention in this world.

 **COUPLES DON'T TEND TO TALK ABOUT SEX UNLESS THEY ARE FIGHTING ABOUT IT.**

You have learned only a skewed view of sex from media, school, and maybe your parents, and now you're in a marriage and in a spot to have sex. Do you feel ready? Where do you get the rest of the story about sex from?

Your spouse! This means you're going to have to talk to your spouse about sex.

Are you comfortable talking about sex with your spouse? I'm a marriage counselor, so I talk about sex almost every day. I tend to be way more comfortable than the couples I'm talking with. **Couples don't tend to talk about sex unless they are fighting about it.** How much communication have you done with your spouse about sex?

Imagine you and your spouse decide to go out for dinner. Here is how it typically goes:

Him: Do you want to out to dinner?

Her: Sure! Where do you want to go?

Him: I don't know, where you do want to go?

Her: I don't really care. Do you want to go to a fast food place or a sit-down meal?

Him: I don't want fast food. I had that twice this week already.

Her: Okay, I'm cool with a sit-down restaurant, where would you like to go?

Him: Don't care, I'm just not in the mood for Mexican. How about seafood?

Her: No, I really don't want that tonight. Just not feeling it. Are you good with Italian?

Him: Sure, that sounds fine. When do you want to go?

Her: Give me 10 minutes, and we can leave.

Look at all that communication just to figure out where you want to have dinner! Do you do the same thing with sex? Why not? I would argue that you care way more about sex than what to have for dinner. If it's more important, shouldn't you talk about it more?

Imagine the above conversation, but instead of dinner this couple was talking about sex. Do you see how healthy that would be and how it would eliminate several problems? Do you talk with your spouse about if you want to have sex, or do you just start putting the moves on them and hope for the best? Do you ask when they want to have sex, or do you just pick when it works best for you or when you're in the mood? Do you talk about what kind? Romantic, slow, quickie, quiet, loud—are you making love or having sex? Has this scenario ever happened:

Him: Do you want to have sex?

Her: Yeahhhh ... if you want.

Him: Never mind.

Her: Why are you upset I said yes?

Him: Forget it.

Her: I'm willing to have sex if you want.

Him: Nah.

Her: Really, why don't you want to have sex? You brought it up. I said yes, and now you don't. What's your problem?

Sex

What is going on here? What changed? He asked to have sex and then changed his mind. Well, neither one of them communicated about what the other was thinking. He apparently felt like she wasn't as excited about sex as he was. She was willing, but not as enthusiastic as he was. He wanted to have passionate sex, and she was thinking of a quieter encounter. If the couple doesn't make communication more important, it's just going to be luck when their preferences do match up. Sometimes it will feel like things are going well, while other times it will feel like things went wrong even when they had the same conversation, and neither knows why.

If you don't talk about sex and just assume you will both be on the same page at the same time, you're just going on what you learned from the media—meaning everything always matches up perfectly when it comes to sex. This will end in a misunderstanding at best and a fight at worst. When a fight ensues is usually the moment couples decide to have a conversation about sex. Things didn't go the way you planned, and you're angry, hurt, disappointed, or embarrassed. This is not the best time to talk about anything. Sex is so powerful that when it goes bad, we tend to cast blame.

If sex doesn't go well, at first spouses tend to blame themselves. We say things to ourselves like, *he doesn't like how I look because I'm not in shape. She doesn't like me because I'm not strong enough.* (Ever notice how when we blame ourselves, we tend to pick the things that are more appearance-based? Weight, height, strength, size?)

If the problem doesn't get fixed by blaming ourselves, then couples will start to blame each other. *Does she never want to*

The Marriage Manual

have sex? He only wants me for sex and doesn't appreciate me! There is always blame going somewhere. If this blame goes on for too long, there can be major problems.

What do you do if the sex life in your marriage has gotten so bad that there's more than just the occasional argument about sex? What happens if most or all of the sex has stopped? If sex has dramatically decreased or stopped, your healthy marriage is in serious trouble. You can still have a marriage. I know some couples who have had little or no sex in their marriage for years. They are still married, but it's not healthy and there's a lot of hurt and blame in the relationship. You must do something different. The best place to start is by acknowledging the mistakes you've made and the pain you've caused your spouse. Review Tool #3: Fighting. Start over. Go slow.

Some couples have been so hurt that they have stopped or rarely have sex, meaning they have most certainly stopped communicating about sex. You want to fix your sex life, but it seems overwhelming and you don't know where to start. You may have tried many times, but most of the time, couples don't start fixing issues at the beginning—they just keep trying to have sex over and over again.

Your spouse has become a stranger if you are not having sex. Intimacy is gone. What is intimacy? Shared feelings. Sex is a way of sharing feelings without talking. That's probably why

 **YOU WILL NEED TO DATE YOUR SPOUSE**

guys like it so much! It's not the only way to share intimacy, and our Tool #2: Communication is the first way you have to share intimacy and the way you will most often share it, but you will need to share intimacy physically as well. If you feel as though your spouse is a stranger, it's likely because you've stopped sharing feelings, leading to them feeling like a stranger. This is also why just trying to have sex will not work. Do you like having sex with someone you have no connection with?

Starting from the beginning means you will need to date your spouse. You will need to start at the beginning and build your relationship back up to the point where you can first talk about sex before having it. What I mean by "date your spouse" is not just going out for dinner and expecting the night to end well. Date them. Spend time with them, talk with them, communicate with them.

Did you have sex with your spouse on your first date? I hope not. Think back to how your dating relationship went. Typically you will date someone a long time before you even start to get close to that person. How many dates/how much time did you spend with your spouse before you kissed them? How much time before you cuddled on the couch? How much time before you made out (And yes, a married couple should still make out!)? Did you talk about it? How did you decide how far to go? Did you have premarital sex? If you look back, hopefully you spent a lot of time learning and talking about each other before things got too physical. This is what I mean by starting from the beginning. You and your spouse need to talk these things through before having sex again.

The Marriage Manual

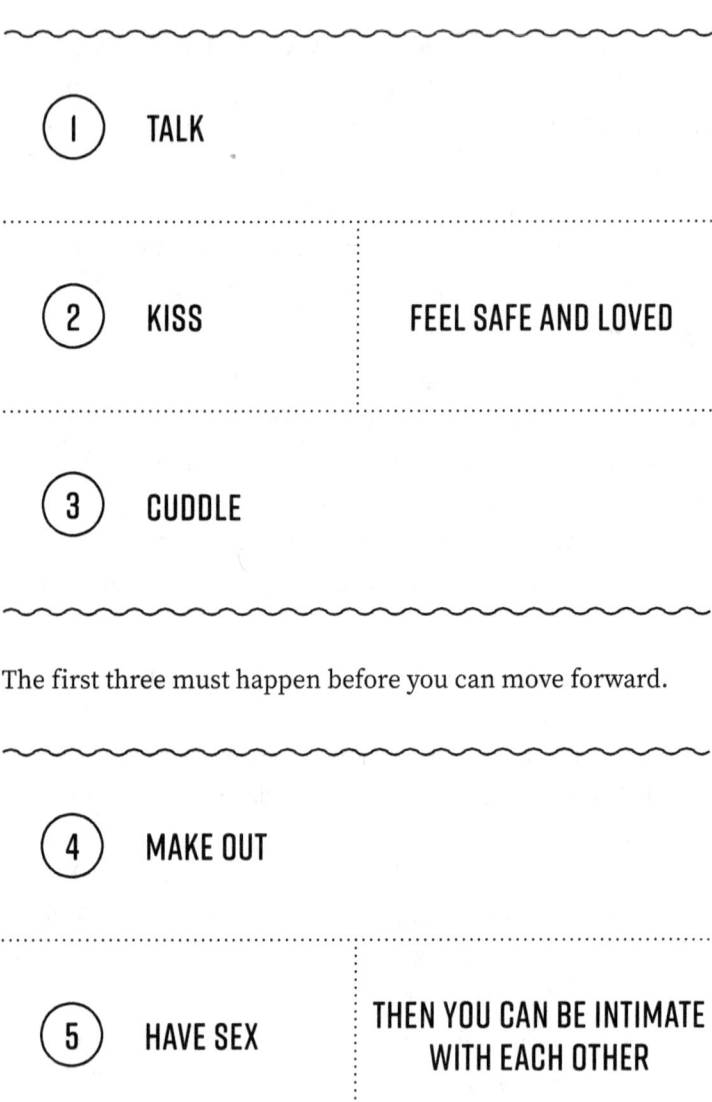

The first three must happen before you can move forward.

You need to do the first three things on this list before the last two can happen. Too often we skip the first four and go straight to sex, especially when things have not been going well. Don't just assume that because you're married you can skip steps. Just because you're married does not mean sex just happens. You and your spouse both need to feel loved (steps 1, 2, and 3) if anything substantial is going to change.

How men and women feel loved is different. I'm tempted to take some time here to explain how men and women are different, but this has been done many times before and better than I could do it. Books like *Men are from Mars and Women are from Venus*[6] or *Men are Waffles, and Women are Spaghetti*[7] both illustrate how men and women are different. I want you to learn these differences about your spouse. These books can give you a good place to start and can help you ask questions and learn about each other, but I want you to learn how your spouse thinks, especially regarding sex in general.

Some generalities about how men and women are different are as follows:

> Women need to feel loved first before they're ready to have sex.
>
> Men tend to have sex first then feel loved as a result.

Your communication with your spouse will need to work this challenge out. How you go about compromising in this area is the work that needs to be done. Remember, like all communication you need to allow your spouse to have emotions and

---

[6] Gray, John. *Men are from Mars, Women are from Venus: A Practical Guide for Improving Communication and Getting What you want in your Relationships.* New York, Harper Collins, 1992.

[7] Farrell, Bill, Farrell Pam. *Men are like Waffles—Women are like Spaghetti.* Eugene Oregon, Harvest House, 2001.

remember that their emotions will be different from yours. In communicating, know that there will be challenges. What happens when your spouse tries to initiate sex and you're not interested? Do you tell them no? Do you walk away mad if you're told no? Is that okay?

 **WHEN YOU TELL YOUR SPOUSE YOU ARE NOT IN THE MOOD...TELL THEM WHEN YOU WILL BE**

Imagine if your spouse asked for sex, you said no, and your spouse replied, "Oh good, I didn't want to have sex anyway. I was just asking because I thought you might want to!" and then your spouse walks away. Are you feeling better or worse now that he didn't get upset about being shut down?

Imagine if your spouse asked for sex, you said no, and your spouse replied, "Oh good, I didn't want to have sex anyway. I was just asking because I thought you might want to!" and then your spouse walks away. Are you feeling better or worse now that he didn't get upset about being shut down?

A straightforward strategy when communicating about sex is to remember that **when you tell your spouse, no, you are not in the mood, tell them when you will be.** When you tell your spouse not tonight because you're tired but that tomorrow night will work because your day will not be as busy, your spouse will be disappointed that it's not happening now, but they will also be thinking about tomorrow night! Get comfortable with communicating about sex. You will, and should, be talking about it for the life of your marriage.

— NOTES —

— TROUBLESHOOTING GUIDE —

AFFAIRS

Affairs can be one of the biggest destroyers of a healthy marriage. Not all marriages survive when an affair happens. This is a difficult situation, and you may need more help than this manual can provide. Counseling is mandatory when an affair has occurred. I've talked to numerous couples who have had an affair who simply did some fighting and then moved on. They didn't know how to or didn't want to deal with all the issues that arise as the result of an affair, and they just got back to doing life and their marriage only to have issues from the unresolved affair surface later on. If you or your spouse have had an affair, please get some help to address what happened. I will give you some basic concepts and ideas to help you begin to deal with an affair in your marriage.

One of the first things when faced with an affair is to identify and recognize your own thoughts. A stumbling block that a spouse will run into are their own thoughts and ideas regarding an affair. It's easy to say, "If he ever cheats, I will leave him." But this becomes a lot harder to do after two kids and eight years of marriage. The spouse who was cheated on will be struggling with what to do—they're torn.

They told themselves that if an affair ever happened they would leave. Now when it actually happened, it's a different story. They've had good times and are in love with the person that hurt them. They have a family. Blowing up a marriage and family now is suddenly hard to do, but they've made this promise to themselves, so they feel trapped. This can make for significant emotional challenges when it comes to knowing how to proceed.

As you're working through what you want to do, be careful of the advice you seek when you're in this confused state. Often your friends and family are sending you the same messages that you told yourself in the past. They haven't taken into account the things that you're now thinking about for the first time. If you can find some spouses who have dealt with affairs and speak with spouses who have stayed and others who have left, that advice is far healthier than someone speaking hypothetically about something they've never experienced themselves. It's easy to find couples who ended their marriage after an affair. It's a little harder to find couples who stayed together, but there are many out there.

Deciding what to do now is your decision. A qualified therapist should not be giving you advice on what to do. The therapist can help you paint a picture of both choices, but in the end it's your decision whether to leave or stay.

If you are the person who had an affair, you also have to wrestle with your previous thoughts about affairs. Often if you have had an affair, you believed that your spouse didn't really care about you. If you have gotten to the point where you're willing to go outside your marriage for love, you have typically told yourself a number of things that allowed you to get to that point. Things like, *She doesn't really love me, He doesn't care about me,* or, *She doesn't even notice if I'm missing from this marriage.*

You have an affair, it gets discovered, and now you see that she is choosing to stay in the marriage. She actually does love you! Your marriage is important to her, you hurt her and then you find out that she loves you more than you thought. Now what? The spouse who had an affair now needs to spend some time figuring out what they want to do. Some spouses decide that they don't deserve to stay married and proceed with divorce out of punishment and shame because they feel like they could never fix their misstep in judgment. Some spouses remain and try to repair the damage. The first place to start when dealing with an affair is yourself. Remember Tool #1.

 Next, you and your spouse need to decide if the affair is done and over. This can be tricky, but too often couples start trying to save a marriage while the affair is still happening or has not completely ended. This may sound crazy, but in the real world it happens often. The wife doesn't want the marriage to end and doesn't want to lose her husband, so she's doing whatever she can to try and save the marriage, which makes total sense but can send the wrong message.

On the other hand, the husband isn't sure if the marriage can be saved and he doesn't want to be alone, so he makes sure he still has options if the marriage ends, which also sends the wrong message. This is what drives couples to therapy. You and your spouse need to both know that the affair is done. If he isn't sure yet, you will have to set some clear boundaries to let him know that a decision needs to be made. This is hard to do because it will feel like everything is out of control, and he may leave you because of that. He might leave, but you can't control that. Your marriage, however, is so special and important that you need to be unwilling to share it, or you're only kind of in a marriage.

If you're the one who had an affair and you haven't ended it yet, just know that the longer you take to decide, the more work you will have to do once you choose, no matter which way you choose. I would encourage you to be ALONE. Don't go back and forth between the two. If you're not spending time with your spouse, and she rightfully said that you need to decide if you want to be in your marriage, it's foolish to make your decision while also talking to the person you had the affair with. Be alone, no contact with anyone, you have a lot of work to do on yourself, and it's your decision alone to make.

Details. They can haunt you. During this time of finding out and deciding if you want to be in or out of your marriage, the spouse who was cheated on often has all kinds of questions. **Be careful what you ask.** There are a number of things that it may at first seem like you need or want to know, only to find out later that these things are just thoughts hanging out in your brain. There are a lot of ways counselors and books about affairs try to handle this dilemma. Some say to write out all your questions and after three months see which ones are still important to you. That sounds great in theory, but when you're scared, hurt, and feeling as though the world is ending, it's difficult to ask someone to pause all the questions you want to ask.

❗ BE CAREFUL WHAT YOU ASK FOR

If I can talk to a spouse early on in the process of an affair, before they've asked their spouse who cheated those questions, I generally advise them to keep their questions initially focused on the broad things, not the details. Finding out what happened is important and needed. What did and did not the affair entail? Which questions do you need answers to now?

What did the affair entail? Talking? Sexting? Dates? Kissing? Sex?

> How often did it happen? One night one time, or multiple times over months?

> Who's the person you had an affair with? A stranger? Co-Worker? Friend?

Initially, be careful with questions that involve details about what exactly happened, as those details tend to stick in your head more than you will want. You may need this information to feel like you can move on, but generally it's best to wait and get a foundation underneath your marriage again. Sometimes when you have that foundation, those details that would get stuck in your brain aren't needed.

If you're the spouse who cheated, your first step is to come completely clean. Don't merely tell part of the story or only tell what your spouse already knows. Often a spouse will make a mistake and think, *She's already mad and hurt, if I tell her the rest of the story she will be gone, so I won't tell her more because it will just hurt her. The affair is done, she knows that, so the rest won't matter.* This kind of thinking is destructive to the marriage. Your spouse typically has just had all the trust taken from her. She doesn't know which way is up, and this is your moment to start new and different. Keeping secrets and not being completely honest is the old way of thinking. If you want your marriage to be unique and different, you need to be new and different. You want to make sure there are no more surprises. Honesty and showing your wife that you want her trust, even when it may destroy your marriage, is a great way to do it differently.

If you're answering your spouse's questions about the affair and you're not sure about something, tell her that. Don't downplay what happened. If she asks you how many times you met up and you don't know if it was three or four times, say four. What you don't want to do is tell your wife it was three times and continue on with your conversation talking about when and where this happened, and your wife says it sounds like it was four. Now she feels like you are still lying and being dishonest with her. This will cause her to think there is more that you're not telling her. She will question you many times when she feels like she can't trust you if periodically you change your story or add to it. Own your mistake. Do not defend it. There are no excuses. You made a bad choice. The best thing you can do is demonstrate that you want to stay married and will no longer be untrustworthy.

One big ramification that impacts a marriage when an affair happens is the choice the spouse who didn't have an affair is forced to make. It's unfair, but this choice needs to be made. The spouse who didn't cheat is suddenly faced with the ques-

Affairs

tion: do you want to stay married? The spouse who has been caught or even simply confessed typically has already made up their mind. They have ended the affair and want to make things work with their spouse. They have maybe even spent a significant amount of time wondering and contemplating what they want to do with their marriage. They have chosen to stay married and work on the marriage.

The other spouse has been blindsided and knocked in the gut with the question. This is not something they've typically been contemplating. Often the spouse who didn't cheat, rightfully so, will be angry and mad that they are even put in this position and have to choose. Their actions didn't put them in this spot, and now their spouse is not only pushing them to choose, but also asking them to choose quickly.

You should take some time to make this choice. Allow time for your emotions to settle, because when you do make this choice, you will need to remind yourself of the choice you made many times. There will be lots of moments going forward where you will wonder, second guess, and be scared. You need to be able to shut some of those fears down by reminding yourself that you have chosen to proceed with the marriage. If you're not sure, don't start doing marriage work. You don't *kind of* want a new marriage—you *really* want a new marriage and will need to be all in. This isn't fair, but if you want the marriage to succeed, you will need to make this choice even though you never asked for the situation in the first place.

If you're the spouse who cheated, you need to know that you also need to change your perspective. Your spouse may take a long time to trust you again. You will be questioned and challenged about where you are or what you're doing. If you see this only as your wife checking up on you or wanting to control you, you will get angry and resentful. You may feel defeated that this is never going to change, and she will hold this over your head forever. If that is the perspective you have, your marriage will be difficult. You will need to change this perspective. You need to focus on yourself, not her. Are you becoming the man and the husband you want to be? Are you acting in a manner that you can be proud of? That needs to be your focus, not whether she's over the past or not. If you can see your wife's questions as not trying to catch you, but as signals that she has triggers and is scared, you will be able to handle the questions better. She isn't trying to catch you having an affair again; she is feeling scared.

Your spouse will be triggered by all kinds of things. Neither of you will be able to see when all the triggers are coming. Some triggers you will be able to see coming, but there will be some that come out of the blue. That is why there will be times when you think you are doing well, and then you will be questioned and you will both feel like you're going backward. If you can see this situation as a trigger where your spouse needs some reassurance and you're still working on being the man you need to be, it will not set you back so far.

At this point the affair had ended, and you're both willing to make a new marriage. The work now begins. As you and your spouse are learning how to communicate again, there is a big idea that you need to remember when communicating: KNOW WHAT YOU ARE TALKING ABOUT!! What I mean is this, are you talking about the affair or your marriage? They are both topics that will need to be talked about and communicated effectively about. The only problem is that you can't talk about them both at the same time, and most couples end up trying to do this.

If you talk about both your marriage and the affair at the same time, your conversations will spin in circles and be painful. This is what I mean, if you're talking about the affair, your wife will be sharing her hurt—emotions, anger, sadness, and frustration will be shared. If you had the affair, there's not much you should be saying other than that you're sorry and owning your mistake. It will be a very one-sided, but needed conversation. If you and your spouse are talking about your marriage and what you want it to look like, if you're the spouse who had an affair, I don't want you to be quiet. I want you to speak up and share what you would like changed about your marriage. If you do that while your wife is talking about the affair, it will sound as though you're blaming her for what happened. That is not a good look. If you have been cheated on and are wanting to talk about how your marriage is going to look and what your spouse wants from the marriage and he is silent and not saying much, you will wonder if he cares or is engaged in making a new marriage. But if he thinks you are talking about the affair and is quiet thinking he is supposed to listen, your conversation could end in a fight.

Couples often, when talking after an affair, will go back and forth talking about both things at the same time. Since there are so many emotions taking place, this is where a lot of the arguments will come from. Go slow and make sure you both know what you are talking about, the marriage or the affair. Both need to be discussed.

Finally, know that it's possible to not only recover from an affair, but also to make a healthy new marriage that both of you cherish. It will take a lot of work. There are a number of things that will need to be figured out, but that feeling of, *when will I be out of the doghouse and an equal member of the marriage again?* and, *when will I ever feel safe and stop worrying about if and when it will happen again?* will pass if you do the work. As I said earlier, get some help from a counselor to guide you through this challenging time.

DOUG AND CARRIE.

Doug and Carrie had been married for 16 years. They had three children. Doug had an affair with someone from the gym. He was caught by Carrie when he wasn't where he was supposed to be. He came clean and shared everything that had been going on. The couple was in crisis, and Doug left to figure things out. Two weeks later, after a number of conversations, Doug came back. He took responsibility for what happened, said he was sorry, and wanted to work on the marriage. Carrie also wanted a new marriage but couldn't move forward as quickly. She struggled with why Doug did this to her. They also lived in a smaller community, and she would run into the person Doug had an affair with around town a lot. This caused many complicated feelings. Carrie had a lot of triggers that would cause her to feel insecure and question her husband's commitment. They were trying to make it work, but were frequently having the same fight over and over. It went like this:

Carrie: I'm having trouble getting over the hurt that you caused me. I have to go about my day thinking about how you lied and were sneaking around. You said you were at the gym, and you were at her house. I have to walk around town feeling like an idiot while you just go about your day. I can't trust you. I don't know what you're doing or where you're at. How do I know you're not going to go back to her?

Doug: I told you I wouldn't go back. I've done everything you asked. I tell you where I'm going all the time. I send you pictures to prove I'm where I say I'm at. I told you I want to make this marriage work. I came back to create a new marriage and make things better. You keep telling me this isn't going to work and you can't do this. I'm here trying to make it work. You keep telling me that I'm not going to change when I have changed, and you haven't.

Carrie: Why do I have to change? I didn't do anything wrong! You did. You're the one who put us in this spot, you need to fix it. You need to make things right.

Doug: I'm trying to make things right. You won't let me. You keep bringing up the past. It was two months ago. I don't go to that gym anymore. I haven't talked to her. I don't have her in my phone or on Facebook. You're the one that keeps looking up what she's doing on Facebook and asking about her. I never bring her up, you always do. You keep bringing her up when I don't want to talk about her. You need to figure out how to move on because if you don't, I don't know how we're going to make it. I have worked really hard to show you that I want to move on with you.

Carrie: Move on!?!? I shouldn't have to be the one moving on! You put me in this spot!

And so it goes on and on, over and over. How do Doug and Carrie get out of this mess? Do you hear how defensive each person is? They're both reacting to what the other is saying. When someone is defensive, they are trying to prove something. What are they trying to prove? Doug and Carrie need to stop trying to blame each other for different parts of the situation. When dealing with such a big hurt, facts are useless. Make the feelings as big as they feel and make the facts small so they don't become a distraction.

> ❗ **IF YOUR SPOUSE STARTS TALKING ABOUT FEELINGS YOU CANNOT SIMPLY JUST START ADDING YOUR FEELING TO THE MIX**

Carrie needs to say less. Her first sentence was okay when she said, "I'm having trouble getting over the hurt you caused me." Adding one more sentence describing that feeling as opposed to jumping to the attack on how Doug is lying and sneaking around keeps the focus on her feelings. How much trouble is she having? If she added the sentence, "I feel like an idiot," now the focus stays on her hurt feelings, and hopefully Doug addresses that.

Now, Doug does have a legitimate feeling that he's trying to share. Did you notice what it was? He's trying to tell Carrie that he has changed and feels as though she does not notice that he's working hard. This is a feeling that will need to be talked about within the marriage but not at the same time that she is talking about feeling hurt and overwhelmed. **If your**

spouse starts talking about feelings, you cannot simply just start adding your feelings to the mix without addressing feelings that have already been shared. Doug needs to bring up that he is feeling like she's not noticing that he is changing, but he shouldn't bring that up now. The reason this fight kept going was because neither person was listening—they both were defending their actions, they were both right and fighting about two things at the same time.

— NOTES —

— TROUBLESHOOTING GUIDE —

ADDICTIONS

One area that can cause trouble for a healthy marriage is addictions. Addictions come in a variety of forms. Most people think about the big three: alcohol, drugs, and gambling. These three are big and have traditionally caused a lot of damage to marriages. Alcohol, drugs, and gambling are usually so big that typically people outside of the marriage can see the impact they are having. These addictions usually continue to grow until they cause so much stress on the marital system that it eventually requires help even if one or both spouses have been trying to avoid getting help.

If you or your spouse has an alcohol, drug, or gambling addiction, you need to seek help from a trusted source, ideally a counselor, AA, or some type of treatment program. If you are the spouse of someone who is addicted, you should do the same. I know their addiction is not your problem, but the problem is usually so big that it has impacted you and your thinking, and outside help is needed. Unfortunately, addiction is one of the few areas where it's difficult to help fix a marriage while an addiction is actively taking place. Most marriage counselors will not work with couples when someone is in the middle of an active addiction. If that person in in recovery, that's a different story.

The simplest way to explain it is, how beneficial do you think marriage counseling will be when one of the participants is high? If you can't do marriage counseling because the person is not all there, that's the same reason you're having trouble in your marriage—your partner is not all there. That doesn't mean that they don't love you, it simply means that before you can figure out if the marriage can be fixed, your spouse needs to be all there. Firm expectations of what you expect and need, and the willpower to stop pretending that things are okay are the best things you can do to help your spouse and your marriage.

There are many more addictions that may not be as initially devastating or happen as fast as the big three, but they can derail a marriage just the same over a more extended period of time. These addictions are not as easily identified. Working too much, spending too much time on social media, being overly involved with your children, playing or watching too much sports, too much time on any hobby, too much volunteering or even working for a good cause—all of these things, when done in excess, can become a hindrance to a healthy marriage. They may not reach the same level of addiction as an alcoholic can, but activities that cause you to reduce the amount of time you're working on your marriage can be damaging.

Your marriage can't always be your top priority even if you want it to be. Life and reality get in the way, but you need to be aware of the other extremes—which are that gradually, over time your activities will take away time that needs to go to your marriage. It's really easy to assume that your marriage will be there when you return from whatever you're doing. Take that approach too often though and it's possible that it won't be, and if it is still there, it will definitely not be in the shape that you left it.

Anything that is important, valuable, and treasured needs to be taken care of. Marriages are no different. You, not your spouse, are responsible for setting boundaries on your activities. It's not your spouse's job to remind you that you've been working late too often or been gone too many weekends. It's also not your spouse's job to tell you to spend less time on your iPad and more time with your spouse. It's your job. It's easy to see the places where your spouse doesn't have balance. It's way harder to see those areas in yourself. We all have things that pull us away from our marriage more than they should. Can you identify those things and set some limits? After you do that, you're in a much better place to address these issues with your spouse.

— NOTES —

— TROUBLESHOOTING GUIDE —

ABUSE

If you have suffered any form of abuse as a child, you need to be aware that it will show up again in your marriage.

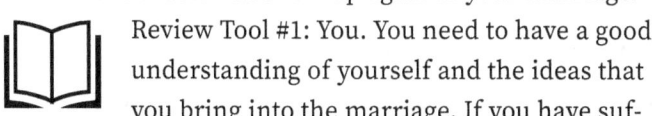

Review Tool #1: You. You need to have a good understanding of yourself and the ideas that you bring into the marriage. If you have suffered from abuse, those ideas are going to be skewed, often wrong, and frequently detrimental to a healthy relationship. Abuse in this context can range from horrific acts done against you, all the way down to simply some poor actions caught up in how your parents raised you. Horrific abuse physically, sexually, or emotionally can leave prominent scars and wounds on your heart that you guard and protect against in future relationships. Even smaller things such as thinking, I know my parents loved me, they just didn't say it that much, can have a big impact on how you approach your marriage. Your approach may be more unhealthy and off way more than you know.

If you were in a situation where you were abused as a child, what conclusion did you come to about yourself? Often these conclusions are not positive. Thoughts like, *I* am no good, I must have done something wrong, I am a bad person, I don't matter, and I am not important, are all natural conclusions to come to. Natural, but wrong. People that experience abuse will carry around those thoughts deep inside their heads long after the abuse has stopped. It was a painful and not fun chapter in their life, so they just try to move on and make the best of things and not think about it too much. They get into a relationship, and now those deep feelings about themselves tend to show up. If you think that you're not important, how will that impact how you treat your spouse? Or how he treats you? If you feel as though you're not valuable, does that impact how you treat your spouse? Meaning, if you don't think you are loveable, are you going to let your spouse love you?

I call these ideas and behaviors your abuse talking. The abuse is telling you things that are not true. The lessons and conclusions you learned when you were younger and getting hurt will repeat themselves in other situations. When you learn to hear your abuse talking, you can also learn to correct it. You will be surprised how often you hear it and how over time, it has just become part of your personality. Even if you wouldn't call the things that happened to you abuse, but just how you were raised. If you grew up in a family where no one ever talked about how loved you were, or if your parents were unable or unwilling to go to activities that you were in, those behaviors can impact how you not only view yourself, but also how you view your spouse. By being aware that you come from some difficult situations and that being in a marriage will sometimes trigger those same feelings, it's important to not only be aware of that, but also know that you will need to do something with those feelings. You will have to change the narrative of how you view yourself.

— NOTES —

— TROUBLESHOOTING GUIDE —

RELIGIOUS DIFFERENCES

This is one of the other big three trouble spots in marriage, meaning that it's something you and your spouse will be talking about as long as you are together—as a reminder, the other two of the big three are sex and money. Like money and sex, your faith is a highly personal matter that you will have strong feelings about. Your faith is personal and important, and you will not like the feeling of something being "wrong" with you that can occur when your spouse has a different religious view. **Your faith means something.** You have a passion for it. When you have a passion, it means you will not like when someone has a different view about your passion. What is your faith? What do you believe? Like we have said before, even in this troubleshooting guide, always go back to your tools. Tool #1: You—know yourself and what you believe and why before discussing religious differences with your spouse.

 **YOUR FAITH MEANS SOMETHING**

Hopefully you don't have big differences in religion, for example one spouse being Christian while the other is Muslim, atheist, or Hindu. Hopefully these differences have been discussed before your got married. If you are married, are you expecting your spouse to change their religious beliefs? Can you each practice your own faith within the context of your marriage? This can cause some significant problems and will most likely illustrate that you need to do a substantial amount of communication because each of you had the idea that your spouse was going to convert but never really spoke about it. It is possible to co-exist with different faiths, but this requires a lot of communication, especially when children become involved.

Hopefully you don't have big differences in your faith/belief systems. Hopefully those differences are simple ones like the differences between Baptist, Catholic, Pentecostal, Methodist, Nondenominational, etc. These smaller differences are to be expected. Remember what you learned previously—your numbers don't match. If they don't match with money and sex, why would they match with your faith? When trying to figure out how to proceed with religious differences, it's helpful to separate this topic into two pieces: tradition and theology. Tradition means what you are used to. Theology is what you believe.

Let's talk about tradition first. Tradition means what are you used to when asked, "what was church like for you as a kid?" Did your church have an organ or a full five-piece band? Did you dress up for church or wear what you wanted? Was your church charismatic or reserved? Was it conservative or contemporary? Then go on to think about what the church you grew up in professed. Infant baptism? Adult baptism? Confirmation classes? Sunday school? How often did your church have Communion, every week or every couple of months? What was your attitude about church attendance? Did you and your family go once a month or two times a week?

All these things form your traditions. These are the things that you gravitate towards. You will tend to feel more comfortable in churches that are more like what you are used to. Now, be careful here, these are important things to think about and take into account when talking about how to compromise and merge with your spouse, but none of these traditional things, although necessary, dictate your theology. Does whether your church have an organ or a band impact whether you go to Heaven or not? How about if you were baptized as a child or an adult? Nope. Often when couples are trying to find a church or working to get their religious beliefs to fall in line with their spouse, they will make the mistake of fighting over tradition things in a way that makes church feel like if it wasn't done a certain way, it's not correct. That's the power of traditions. They make us feel comfortable and safe, but we also assume that our way is the only way to do something or the only right way—we always do it like this, so it must be right.

It is right ... to you, not necessarily to your spouse. While you each may believe that Jesus saved both of you, your spouse has their own thoughts and traditions that they are equally passionate about. If you and your spouse spend your time trying to convince each other who is more passionate or whose traditions are right, you will be in for a lot of fighting that may never end. It may even get to the point where you just stop talking about your faith altogether.

With theology, you will find that you often don't disagree as much as you think. When talking about theology, you don't need a theology degree or to make it too deep or analytical. Keep the conversation authentic and real. What do you believe? How are you saved? Remember Tool #3: How to fight. Remember to start where you agree and work on the problem from that perspective. In terms of faith, it's helpful to have Jesus as an absolute. Meaning, you are saved if you ask Jesus into your life. That's it. Pretty much every form of Christianity holds that view. That's what I mean by that belief being absolute. That is absolutely necessary. After that, things start to get gray very fast. How you proceed after you are saved is the basis for all the different denominations and beliefs. Churches are basically saying this is how we think you should respond to the fact that Jesus saved you. Because he saved you, we think you should act and behave in this manner. This is powerful, and when Jesus comes into your life it will be so powerful and magnificent that your life should change and be different. What that difference means and looks like is different for different churches, people, and your spouse. That difference can be worked on and negotiated. You need to know what you believe and why you do what you do. Why are you acting the way that you are acting? Why are you acting differently? If you don't know this, be careful because you just took your belief and made it a tradition, and you don't understand why. The best example I can use to illustrate this concept comes from my own upbringing.

I grew up in a traditional conservative church. It had a lot of rules. Most of them never bothered me as a kid growing up, which is another way of saying I didn't spend too much time thinking about the rules. When I became a teenager, of course, I started to question the rules. The main rule I questioned was my church's and my parents' rules about what I could and couldn't do on Sunday and how we always had to dress up.

I was not allowed to do a lot of things on Sundays. There were a number of things that my family didn't do on Sunday. When I was little, I would ask why we couldn't go swimming or fishing on Sunday and my parents would say, "We can't because it's Sunday." When you're 10 years-old, that answer works. When you're 16 and want to play soccer with your friends, you start to question the rule.

I questioned my dad on why we couldn't do things on Sunday. He gave me a great answer that I finally understood. He said it was our way of making Sunday special and different. "Sunday needs to be a day set apart from the other days. By not doing everything that you normally do, it is a way of setting Sunday apart to honor God."

I asked him, "Can't I play soccer on Sunday and honor God?"

He replied, "I don't know, can you?"

My dad is a brilliant man. We talked, and I told him what things I would do or not do to make Sunday special. He listened and told me I could play as long as I did the things that I said I would to make the day different and special and not miss church. I could play. Since we were talking, I had one more question: "Why do I always have to dress up for church?" We always had to wear nice, "dressy" clothes.

He said, "Don't you want to look nice for God? When you go out on a date or hang with your friends, don't you always wear your favorite things? Why wouldn't you want to do the same for God?"

I was now more aware of what I was doing and not doing on Sundays, and when I was getting ready for church, I was now dressing in a way to try and honor God with respect. The point of the story is you need to know why you are doing what you are doing. When you know, it has more meaning and purpose, but you can also be flexible. I'm pretty sure my dad didn't like me playing soccer on Sundays and wearing a nice shirt paired with jeans, but he knew my heart and what I was trying to do, which is precisely what he was trying to teach me. He would never dress my way or do those types of things on Sundays that I did, but it wasn't about the rules, it was about the meaning behind them. You need to be able to do this with your spouse when talking about the things you believe in.

Religious differences can be hard to navigate because we're passionate, and they have a deeply profound significance in our life. Knowing what you believe and what you are trying to accomplish, and being aware that your spouse has the same overall goal, will help you navigate this difficult topic.

— NOTES —

— NOTES —

— TROUBLESHOOTING GUIDE —

MENTAL HEALTH ISSUES

Mental health issues in marriage can happen to anyone at any time. They can certainly impact your marriage. There is a big stigma with mental health issues. No one thinks twice about going to the doctor for a physical health issue. If you have an ankle problem, you go to the doctor. The fix can simply be to stay off your ankle for a couple days and ice and evaluate it, all the way up to surgery and crutches for a number of weeks. No one scoffs at you or second guesses why you did what you did when it comes to a physical injury, they just offer support and move on.

The same should be done with mental health issues. Sometimes the healing is short and doesn't take much time, and sometimes it's a bigger issue, takes longer, and has a more significant impact on your life. Taking away some of the stigma allows for people to be more willing to ask for help and seek it out, whether this is for you or your spouse in marriage. It's not helpful to anyone if you simply decide to limp around on your ankle and let it keep hurting you—it is also not wise to let mental health issues go untreated.

Anxiety and depression are like the sprained ankles of mental health. They are pretty common, and at some point you will have some of those feelings. Knowing that having excess worry or sadness is something that everyone experiences from time to time will be important to remember when you or your spouse are going through a time of anxiety or depression. Most people will only experience mild symptoms, and they can usually identify what the cause is for those symptoms. Some people will have more significant levels of depression and anxiety, which may require counseling or medication. If you are the person suffering from those symptoms, remember that your spouse is going through them as well. Often the person having the struggle themselves is not enough of a push to get help, but when they realize that their mental health issues are also impacting their spouse or their children, then they are ready to seek help so their mental health doesn't hurt the ones they love. Remember, your moods impact your marriage. If you are the spouse of someone who is struggling, support them and encourage them to seek help and not to simply deal with it or suck it up. Sometimes sharing how their mental health issues get in the way of having the marriage that you want can be powerful if done in a way that is not blaming.

Sometimes in a marriage, you or your spouse will have a bigger challenge than everyday mood struggles. Major mental health issues that cause significant dysfunction in how an individual manages daily life can really challenge a marriage. When someone has a serious mental health issue, it causes an imbalance in the marriage relationship. This imbalance needs to be stabilized. Someone who is acting in a manner that is

❗ ANXIETY AND DEPRESSION ARE LIKE THE SPRAINED ANKLES OF MENTAL HEALTH

not healthy for them, let alone their marriage, will cause the other spouse to feel helpless and not know how to manage the erratic behaviors that are coming their way. Being clear with your spouse about what you think is happening and how their actions are a result of them having some mental health challenges is not an easy conversation to have, but talking about it in a way that shows you are trying to help and make things better is needed.

Difficult conversations are mandatory for a healthy marriage, the subject of mental health is no exception. Talking about how the behaviors of the dysfunctional person and how those behaviors impact the marriage must be addressed. Talking about mental health using the metaphors of a hurt ankle or some other physical health impairment can help take the sting out of the discussion. Talking with your spouse and looking at it like an old injury that has been present for a long time and is now getting worse, or something new that just started happening is helpful. Getting the perspective from both of you will be helpful. Does only one of you see the mental health issue as something that needs to be addressed, or are you both on the same page? What is the treatment plan? Often couples will have a good conversation about this subject only to come to the conclusion that there is a problem but settle with that fact that there's nothing they can do to fix it.

The Marriage Manual

You may not always be able to fix a mental health issue, but you can still make a plan to deal with it. Finally, if you or your spouse has some significant mental health challenges, don't be afraid to seek help in counseling, either individual, joint, or both to help treat the challenges.

Mental Health Issues

— NOTES —

— NOTES —

— TROUBLESHOOTING GUIDE —

MARRIED LATER IN LIFE

If you marry later in life, hopefully you have matured over time, and this will help you avoid some of the challenges that young couples experience. You should have healthier self-esteem and confidence in knowing that you can live life on your own. You have the ability to be self-sufficient, independent, and successful. That is great. Those are also the things that can make living with someone else more challenging. You know how to do things your way, and you have the experience to prove that your way works. The problem comes in when your spouse has the same experiences and thinks that their way works as well—we have learned many times already that those ways probably don't match.

If you're married after spending some time alone, it will be important to make sure you approach all the conversations about how you want your marriage to work with the perspective that your spouse has already been living life successfully without you, so your spouse does not NEED your ways and may not even WANT your ways of doing things. Taking extra time to look at the roles, expectations, and responsibilities of living together and finding out how your spouse did life before they met you will reduce the number of arguments.

One area where this is especially important is in living arrangements. Often both spouses may have an established place of living. Take the extra time to talk about what your living situation looks like after marriage. Are you moving into his house? Is he moving into yours? Are you buying a new one together? If you're selling one of your houses, what are you doing with the money from the sale? It's important, regardless of what you do, to make whatever place you choose to live your home. If you are moving into one of your homes, your spouse needs to already have established what you guys are going to do to make it feel like you have a place there. Repainting, redecorating, and getting new furniture are things that couples have done to make the other spouse feel welcome. There have been numerous times where I will hear someone talking in counseling about not feeling like they matter in the marriage and go on to hear a story where a spouse moved in and felt as though they "messed up" the other person's house. I listen to them say, "I was allowed one room, a chair, and part of the garage." Does that sound like a partnership? Being sensitive to new living arrangements will help you get off on the right foot.

When you've been living on your own, you will have a number of goals that you've already started working on. You may be working on a promotion that will have you moving to a bigger city. Is your spouse aware of this? You may have been saving money for a couple years to take a trip to Europe. Is your spouse aware of this? What happens when you get married, and the money that you thought was going to that trip now goes to pay off his credit card debt? All these problems are solvable. They just take healthy communication and the sharing of dreams, fears, and goals. Just like anyone else who gets married, the only difference when getting married later in life is you are just a little further along on your way to meeting your goals.

JIM AND PAM.

Jim was 32 years-old, worked in an office, and owned his own home. Pam was 29 years-old and a nurse. She had a twin home and rented out the other side. Jim and Pam met through some mutual friends. They dated for 10 months then got married. Pam sold her twin home and moved into Jim's house. They came into counseling because they had frequent arguments, and both of them felt like things were never getting resolved. They would just fight about something, it would die out, and then they would simply move on. Jim and Pam would fight about lots of things. They fought about how she came in and took over his house. Pam was frustrated that she could never make changes in Jim's house without talking to him first. One of the fights that they had in the counseling session was about getting a new car.

Pam: My lease is almost up, and I want to trade my car in and get a different car, and Jim won't let me.

Jim: She's over on her miles, and it makes more sense just to get out of the lease by buying the car. A lease is a dumb idea in the first place. We would be losing money if she just went and got a lease again. I never lease cars. It doesn't make much sense. You should never lease a car. She doesn't understand how financially it's a bad decision.

Pam: See what I mean? I've been leasing cars for five years. It works just fine. Yes, it may cost a little more, but I never have to worry about car repairs or having to fix it if something goes wrong. It makes my life simple.

Jim: It doesn't cost a little more, it costs a lot more. There's no need for it. It doesn't make any sense. Why would you not just buy a car? Then you don't have to worry about how many miles you put on it. You don't lose money on it when you trade it in, and you can save money by driving for more than a couple of years. This makes the most sense. I've had my truck for six years, and I don't owe any money on it.

This couple was stuck trying to show that their way was right. The crazy thing was that they're both correct. Jim's way of buying a truck did save money and made a lot of financial sense. He didn't mind driving older vehicles and felt satisfied when he had them paid off. Pam, on the other hand, liked having different cars every couple of years. She also really liked the fact that she never had to worry about fixing her car if something went wrong. The idea of a lease provided a sense of comfort and variety for Pam. If she had to pay a little extra for that, it was worth it to her.

Both ideas have been proven to work for each of them. It's only natural to want to keep doing your idea that works well and isn't broken, why would you change it? Jim needs to remember what the goal is in this conversation. Is the goal to validate and prove your way is right, or is it to show that you want to love and support your wife? Proving your way (sometimes your way is your way of life) works is not the point. What is the goal? Helping your spouse. These types of arguments are common when you have been living successfully on your own. Eventually, Jim could see that Pam didn't blow money frivolously and had been successful before he came into the picture. He learned to see that the goal was to help his wife get a car without having to worry about fixing it. Pam was able to agree that she would buy the car, and he would deal with it when it didn't work. They also decided that she would be trading the car in not when it died, but every couple of years.

— NOTES —

— TROUBLESHOOTING GUIDE —

STEP-CHILDREN

This is one of the biggest challenges that I have seen couples face in trying to have a healthy marriage: the presence of step-children. It's typically a second marriage for one or both spouses. Hopefully you have spent some time using Tool #1 to learn about you and the reasons your first marriage didn't work, and that work has already been done by you and your spouse. But dealing with the reason the first marriage didn't work out will not make coping with step-children easier. It's hard enough with step-kids, so you'll want to try and reduce as many of the challenges right away. Therefore, having you and your spouse on the same page is absolutely mandatory when bringing step-children into the mix. This is challenging because you're making a new family while you're also making a new marriage.

There are several issues with creating a new family. Things like, what is your role with the step-kids? How do you respond when you're told that you're not their mom or dad? How do you treat your own kids versus your step-kids? These are challenges you will face, but they're not necessarily within the scope of this book. I'm going to try to keep the focus within the realm of marriage here. A number of these issues will most likely need to be addressed in family meetings and counseling if needed.

When talking to your spouse about step-children and parenting, it's important to, like in affairs, know what you're talking about. Are you talking about marriage issues or parenting issues? These two can easily get combined, making things even more difficult. When talking about your marriage, make sure you do lots of reassuring that you and your spouse are good. Meaning, the marriage is healthy and strong even if our step-parenting skills are not. Reassurance that you are still a good husband or wife while talking about your challenges as a step-parent is important. This is important because there will be many more times when you will feel like you're failing as a step-parent. Knowing that you're not failing as a spouse too will help during this time of learning.

 **DON'T BLAME EVERY PROBLEM YOUR FAMILY IS HAVING BECAUSE IT IS A BLENDED FAMILY**

It's also important when talking about step-parenting to view your role from a healthy perspective. Oftentimes step-parents label every challenge they're facing as a result of being in a blended family, when sometimes the challenges are simply normal family challenges. Children are hard to raise. Parents will always have different parenting styles and skills regardless of if the family is blended or not. **Don't blame every**

problem that your family is having on being a blended family. The more you can find normalcy in your situation, the better. Ask yourself, is this still a *problem you would be having if your family was not blended?* You will be surprised by how often the answer is yes. Solving parenting differences is something you have to do, whether this is the first marriage, or the second, or the third.

A helpful hint to remember in step-family situations is this: remember the kids. The kids will come before the marriage. This is not ideal. It's hard enough to remind a couple when they have biological children not to put them first over the marriage. It's difficult, and at best, couples can usually only do this for periods of time before they return to putting the children before the marriage. It's almost impossible to do so in a blended family. That is the reality. You are going to choose your children over your spouse, and your spouse will do the same. Instead of pretending this does not exist, it's helpful to acknowledge and even communicate about how this tendency shows up and impacts your marriage.

The best advice in this situation is to tell couples to not put your spouse in a situation where your they feel like they need to choose between the marriage or their children. If you work together and are aware of the situation, you can avoid this. By working hard to not ever put your spouse in a spot where they have to pick you over their own children, you can eliminate a number of struggles that blended families face. Often couples spend so much time fighting that they just get stuck. Working to avoid challenging situations that neither of you wants to be in is way more productive than just saying the situation should not be this way.

Another helpful hint for step-children is knowing your role. In this blended family, you typically know your role with your own children, you probably **know your role** as a spouse, but the role of step-parent is most likely new and different and you don't have much experience with it. Remember, you are not their parent. You are their step-parent. What does that look like? You aren't their mom, but you will be doing a lot of mom jobs. You aren't their dad, but you will be doing a lot of dad things. What does being a step-parent look like to you, and what is your step-child/step-children's idea of what that would look like? As a step-parent, you need to learn how to be supportive, helpful, and a resource, all while respecting the boundaries of the step-child and their biological parent(s). This requires a lot of healthy ongoing communication, it's definitely not something that's talked about just once.

Lastly, remember that you are creating a new family, not replacing the old one. That needs to be communicated to your spouse first and the children second. Having this perspective of creating another family when everyone is together at the house that you and your spouse run helps everyone realize what is expected. Hopefully you can reduce the number of times you and the kids think this isn't how they used to do it. That's probably correct, but you're not trying to add children or spouses into your current family or your previous family habits. You are creating a different family, which means it will be different than anything you, your children, your spouse, or your spouse's children have ever been part of. It's not mandatory that the rules in one family be the same as in others. When your step-children are visiting or living with the other parent and they come back to your house, you don't have to have the same rules and expectations as they have with their other family.

If you can keep those hints in mind, it will make your job at a step-parent easier, but not easy. Being a step-parent to your spouse's children, if done well, can be a powerful way to communicate to your spouse how much you love and appreciate them.

PART 3

ROUTINE MAINTENANCE

— NOTES —

— PART 3 —

ROUTINE MAINTENANCE

To get the most out of your healthy marriage, you will need to do some routine maintenance to make sure it keeps functioning at peak performance. Just like anything else that you have a manual for, you will need to do some routine maintenance for your marriage. Think about your TV. Sometimes you will get an alert that it needs a software update. That's easy. Just hit a button, and everything upgrades. Other times the maintenance is a little more invasive, and it means taking the TV off the wall and bringing it to the shop to get a component fixed. Once fixed, the TV is good as new! Marriages are much the same—some things aren't too hard to do to keep things going well, and some take a little more time and effort to get a marriage back to running smoothly

If you feel like your marriage has been running smoothly but has recently been a little sluggish or will freeze up from time to time, it may simply need an update. Software updates are done just to keep things going well. An update typically doesn't take much time and, pretty quickly, things are running as intended. How do you know when you need an update? When you're starting to feel alone or disconnected.

Perhaps you and your spouse have been unusually busy with work and family challenges (sickness, travel, etc.), and you haven't had time to connect. Don't get lazy, if you wait too long you will have to do some serious maintenance to repair the marriage. I want you to be aware that things happen, but they are not necessarily signs that your marriage is bad or going downhill. There will be times in your marriage where you will need to simply reboot, get focused, and resume your efforts, and things will then settle back into a good routine.

One of the easiest things to do to maintain your marriage is to take some time together. Taking a few minutes to talk just to get reconnected is highly beneficial. Couples will often miss this step and try to jump right into the next thing they need to address, simply assuming their spouse will be okay and understand the challenges occurring. Or they will jump directly to trying to have sex and connect that way, which also has its complications. Taking 15 minutes to go for a walk or just kicking all the kids out of a room can reboot things quickly.

Another simple thing to do to reboot is to go big on the positives. Get your spouse's attention by simply praising them for the things that they are doing. Find the positive and praise the positive, no matter how small it may be. It's helpful to share why you're sharing the positives. You can say, "I'm trying to point out the good things you do because I haven't always noticed all the good things you do and I'm feeling far away from you," or, "I miss you, and I'm trying to show you how much I love you." I will let you choose which way you want to tell your spouse why you're sharing positives.

One last thing you can do for a simple reboot is participate in marriage workshops or retreats. These are great ways to get refocused and reconnected with your spouse. If you go to workshops or retreats before things are in crisis mode, they can be enjoyable and feel like a vacation and not like you are being sent to the principal's office.

Remember when you start to see and feel the signs that things aren't running right, don't just think they will get better without any intervention. Just like a computer or a phone, don't avoid the updates on your marriage until something is wrong.

When doing routine maintenance, you need to be aware of where your marriage is at in its life cycle. Are you a newlywed? In the middle of it with kids? Empty nesters? Retirement? Marriage will need different things depending on where the marriage is at.

If you're in the beginning stages of your marriage, routine maintenance will be essential. You're trying to set up good routines and patterns that you can do for your lifetime. You're going to work hard to make sure you're not creating any bad habits that will get bigger over time. Taking time to communicate, talk, and check-in should be done frequently. The things that are talked about later in this section will need to be done often, and probably scheduled so you make an intentional effort to complete them.

If you are in the middle of your marital life stage, hopefully you have routines and good habits established. Your challenge now is how to keep doing these things when you don't have the time or energy to put into them. Finding ways to streamline your maintenance and do it quickly and efficiently is important. This is the season when marital satisfaction drops quite a bit. You will need to keep doing maintenance because your marriage is under stress. Think about a car that drives a few hundred miles a year and a truck hauling a heavy load daily. Which one needs more oil changes and maintenance? When your marriage is in this middle stage, it's no different. Do the maintenance now so it doesn't break down.

If you're in the empty nest or retirement stage of your marriage, you should have a good idea of what things work the best for you. What do you find most enjoyable? You should be able to identify when you need to do some maintenance just by feelings. You won't need to schedule it, you will be able to identify the signs that mean it needs to be done. You and your spouse will both work together to identify when things need to be done or addressed, and it probably won't even feel like work.

Maintenance will need to be done at all stages, just with different priorities and challenges. Maintenance will take time and energy. Don't skip it just because it will take time. A little prevention is worth a lot on the back end to reduce potential problems.

NO LEFTOVERS!

Time is tricky. We often use it poorly and in the wrong ways. Think about your average day. What time of the day are you at your best? Where you are when you're at your best, what are you doing? For most people, their best times are when they're away from their spouse, not with them. You're at work, being productive, doing the business things of the day, succeeding at all your tasks, handling challenges—you may even have time to send a text to your spouse telling them you love them and can't wait to see them. When do you finally see them? When do you have time to talk with your spouse? Usually it's at the end of the night when you have nothing left to give. Now the loving, fun ideas and thoughts that you had at 11am are gone. Now you're simply trying not to fight with your spouse and just fall asleep. Your spouse gets the leftovers. **No leftovers**. Repeat this process enough times, and you will stop sending those texts and won't even reach out to your spouse. This is actually how a lot of affairs start—you're spending your time with other people who are at their best, giving their best to others, and that looks attractive and desirable.

One way to get around this time problem is to communicate with your spouse during your breaks and text them when you're at your best. Now, here's the catch: texting feelings doesn't work very well. You can't communicate feelings via text very well. Emojis help, but not usually enough. Also, when you share a feeling and your spouse doesn't respond for a couple hours, it tends to feel hurtful even when it's not meant to be.

If you're going to communicate with your spouse and you shouldn't communicate a lot of feelings, what should you be communicating? Communicate facts. Deal with issues you're going to have to talk about anyway. Dealing with "business of the family" during the day is a fair use of time. It's stuff you will have to talk about eventually, and if you can get it done during the day you can carve out more time for sharing feelings when you get home. What is the "business of the family?" Things like, what is the plan tonight? Who is going where? What activities do you have? Who is picking up the kids? What errands need to be run? Who is going to do what? These are all things that will need to be talked about. If you wait till the end of the day, by the time you get those things done you will most likely fall asleep. Text facts and plans, not feelings or relationship issues. Too often when you're away from each other, spouses will send texts and try to resolve fights from the night before. It's tough to read emotion into a text. Is your spouse trying to resolve the fight or continue it? You will read it one way, and they will read it a different way.

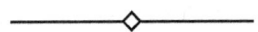

The first big thing when talking specifically about routine maintenance is making sure to have check-ins. Checking in with your spouse on how the marriage is doing is important. Don't check in on work, kids, money, etc., but check in specifically on your marriage and how you're doing as a spouse. When did you last ask your spouse how you're doing in terms of being a husband or wife? Taking some time to talk specifically about the marriage will provide a number of positive benefits.

One way you can do this is by asking your spouse what grade you have earned this past week in marriage.

 ## WHAT GRADE DID YOU EARN THIS WEEK IN MARRIAGE?

Do you remember when you were in school, and the teacher passed back your test grade? If you were like me, if it was a good grade I would leave the test out on my desk face-up so all could see. If it was a bad grade, I would flip it over so no one would see. This same scenario can also happen as an adult with performance evaluations, corrective action plans, or yearly reviews. These things now have fancy names, and salary and bonuses are sometimes attached. But remember how good you feel when you get a good report and how bad you feel when you get a bad report. Some of the most important things in life we never get graded on, such as marriage. Think about how much harder you would be working on your marriage if you got a grade on it. Would you be leaving it out on your desk for all to see, feeling proud of the work you have done, or would you flip it over and hope no one notices that you didn't do your best?

We tend to work harder if we know we're getting a grade on something. What grade would your spouse give you for the past week of marriage? How about the past month? Do you know what's on your spouse's grading scale? What grade would you give yourself? Giving a grade is a good starting point to keep the communication going. If your spouse gave you a B, why did she give you a B? What did you do above average? What did she appreciate? If she gave you a D, where are you lacking? Is this a grade for overall behaviors, or just reflective of one incident? What grade does your spouse get? What's your average together? Use this grade idea as a way of giving a report on how things are going and where you need work. Rember how great it will feel when your spouse gives you an above-average grade on loving them.

Another good check-in is checking where you're sleeping at night. Are you and your spouse sleeping in the same room? If not, what's the reason? Lots of couples will move to different bedrooms when they have a fight, stay there for a while, and then move back. Sometimes they stay in separate rooms even after a fight is over. Sometimes couples will move to a different room when someone is sick and never come back. Sometimes a spouse will put a child to bed and stay in their child's room, neither spouse says much, and now it's a pattern. They are not in the same room and they don't say too much about it.

Don't pretend that things are okay. If you and your spouse are not sleeping in the same bed, something isn't good in the marriage. As a general rule, if you leave your bed, you better inform your spouse why you left and when you plan on coming back. If and when you go back to the marital bed, you better tell them why. This should make both of you aware of why you're doing what you're doing. What are you trying to accomplish? Just sending the message to your spouse that you are unhappy is not a bad thing if your spouse knows that's why you're doing what you're doing. How is your spouse interpreting what you're doing? Do they see it as you letting them know you're hurt and not okay, or do they see your behavior as you trying to punish them or manipulate them to try and get your way? Just leaving the bedroom is not enough. Stalemates can happen where both spouses feel frustrated because the other spouse is not responding to their actions, so they just quit trying to resolve it. Communication needs to accompany the behavior of sleeping somewhere else.

The next big check-in is checking in on how you're coming on your marriage goals. Periodically reviewing your progress on your marital goals is a great way to check in on how your marriage is doing. Don't have a marriage goal? What?! Why not?! Think about it, most couples don't have a marriage goal. It's probably the one area of your life where you don't have goals. What's your goal for your career? Most people have a pretty good plan of what they want to do. If you're a plumber, you start as a journeyman, then work your way to an apprentice, then you're a plumber, you will work for a company for a while and then maybe have your own shop one day. If you're a nurse, you will work nights in a hospital, then work your way up to a day shift, then maybe to a clinic, perhaps even go back to school to become a nurse practitioner. Even if you're a stay-at-home mom, you have career goals surrounding home school or volunteering or having a part-time home business. You also have other goals that are for your family. You and your spouse most likely have housing goals about renting or buying a house, then upgrading your house, maybe adding a camper or even a lake home! You will have goals for when to have children, like being married for three years then having two kids about three years apart. All your goals may not be achieved or happen precisely how you want, but you have them.

Now, what about your marriage? No goals?! Not good. Have you noticed that if people don't have marriage goals, they are actually going backward? Meaning they start at the highest point and go downwards, not upwards. Couples will fall in love and then try and make the honeymoon phase last as long as possible. Then they say, well, the honeymoon is over. The couple will then try to get through having children and hopefully still like each other after the kids have left, then fear retirement when you have more time with your spouse, but you'll hopefully hang on and tolerate your spouse till you die! What type of goal and plan is that?! Unfortunately, that is what many couples have for goals. They end up treating their spouse as someone who is just hanging out with them. Once they're married, they have the view that all the work is done. If that is your goal, no wonder your marriage is struggling.

When you get hired for a job, can you imagine telling your boss, "I'm going to give you two to three great years, then I'm going to just go through the motions for about 18-20 years because I will have other more important priorities, and then if you're lucky I will put a little more effort in for a few years until I can't stand it anymore and just coast out till I retire!" Obviously that would not go well for your job. Your marriage is no different.

Create some marriage goals. Sometimes the question alone will spark some great talks with your spouse. What kind of marriage do you want? What does a good marriage look like? Do you want the same marriage as your parents have? Why or why not? Start to think about what it means to have a good or healthy marriage and what that all entails. It should be fun to think about. What qualities or characteristics do you want your marriage to have? What would you like it to look like in five years, 10 years, 35 years? Go ahead and dream for the lake home! What does the "lake home" marriage look like? Have a fun dream and talk to your spouse to find out what they are thinking as well. Have some marriage goals. Don't worry if you don't have goals right away, take time to figure them out. At first this process will look like check-ins to develop some goals. Check-ins are important and will help keep you working towards the goals.

The next big thing you need to do for routine maintenance is bring power and meaning to the thousands of "little things" you and your spouse do together. This makes up the majority of the time that you will spend with your spouse. Below are all things that you will do with your spouse frequently during the marriage. Bring meaning to these things. That means putting significance and power into the little activities that you do with and for your spouse all the time.

1. **Date night:** You will hopefully have these. Make sure you call it "date night" or else it simply turns into going out to eat. You will have those moments when you just go out to eat or go to an activity, but as soon as you call it a date night, little things start to happen. You change your clothes before you go out. You pick a different place to eat. You smile and look at your spouse a little more just because it's called date night. You act different, usually better. You and your spouse will need to talk about how often you want to have a date night. There will be periods during your marriage where time, money, and babysitters will impact the frequency of your date nights, but you still need to

have a date night. Make it a priority. Never cancel date night. You may have to postpone it, but don't cancel.

2. **Downtime together:** Bring meaning to those times when you're just together and don't have big plans. Are you laying on the couch vegging out, or are you watching a Netflix series together? Make rules that you're not allowed to watch the show without the other person present. This little change now puts some togetherness even into watching TV as opposed to just seeing what's on and killing some time watching a basketball game or game show and then going to bed.

3. **Playing games:** This is often overlooked, especially with all the electronic alternatives out there today. Playing a board game sounds silly, but you will be surprised by how much talking and communication occurs while playing a game. Electronic games work as well, but you will notice that there will be a little less talking due to the screen interaction. Finding other couples to play some cards with is also a great way to keep the marriage healthy.

4. **Take a walk:** Not for exercise, but to talk. Maybe the better word would be take a stroll. Walking just spurs talking, especially if you're not trying to get a specific distance in a certain amount of time, but are simply using talking as something to do while walking. It doesn't have to be long. Just don't make walking a race or make it feel like exercise. If you want to exercise with your spouse, go ahead, just don't combine the two.

5. **Shared activities:** A mission trip where you and your spouse have a joint goal of what you want to do, see, or accomplish can be a great time where you're talking about shared ideas and goals. Hobbies that you both enjoy can be great ways to spend some time together and check in with each other at the same time.

Another way that you can do a more formalized approach to routine maintenance would be by attending counseling or marriage retreats. Like I've said before, something doesn't have to be wrong for you to see a counselor. Some couples come in to check in on how their communication is doing, or get some new ideas on how to approach or handle situations. If you think there may be a problem or you're even having a fight that doesn't ever seem to get resolved, go in and see a counselor. Early intervention is always best. Think about healthcare. When do you want to go see a doctor, when you have a small spot on your leg that needs to be removed or when cancer has spread, and you have to have your whole leg amputated? It's the same with counseling. It's easier to come in when you're stuck over an argument that you can't seem to get resolved, or you can wait five years and then have to deal with hurt, resentment, and wondering how much you care about each other. Often couples will wait till later. When that happens, it takes a lot of counseling just to get a couple to see that their marriage is worth saving and that they do still care about each other, it's only then that you can finally start working on the problem.

One last way to do routine maintenance on your marriage is to go on vacation. Not a family vacation, those tend to help spouses work on their problem solving and communication

The Marriage Manual

skills (😊), but on a vacation with just your spouse. Going on vacation is a great way to see that you and your spouse are on the same page. A vacation can remind you and your spouse of why you're doing all this work in the relationship. Most couples can do vacations well. You could make the argument that if you didn't do a vacation well together, you and your spouse have some severe issues that you should work on immediately. Couples typically do well on vacations because vacations highlight some of the tasks needed to make a marriage go smoothly. When a couple goes on vacation, they must have a conversation about where they want to go, how much they want to spend, what type of activities they want to do. They need to agree on the goals mutually. The goals, in this case, are usually pretty straightforward—the goal on most vacations is to relax and have fun. There are also usually very few distractions on vacation. You both have the same goal, and there are very few distractions, so it tends to be a good setup for success. Your vacations can be big (a week in Mexico), medium (a weekend away), or a small dinner and walk in the park while the kids are at grandma's. Smart couples know how to make the short outings count as much as the big vacations. These vacations can be a good reminder of how you and your spouse are capable of working together and having a good time. If you can work through all the steps for a good vacation but return home and the old ways and patterns remerge, you now have a chance to identify them better and try to do things like you did them while you were on vacation.

Routine Maintenance

— NOTES —

PART 4

WARRANTY INFORMATION

— NOTES —

— PART 4 —

WARRANTY INFORMATION

When you buy a new TV, it typically has a limited warranty. You usually have to register where you purchased it, keep the information about where you bought it, and save the receipt. The good news is your marriage also comes with a limited warranty. Just like any other warranty, you need to register and do your part for it to work. This is a limited warranty. You will not get your money back if your marriage is not working and no trade-ins are accepted. I would have been traded in long ago if that was allowed! The warranty is simply a way of increasing your chances of success, and when things go totally off the rails, you will hopefully be given an opportunity to restore or save it.

How do you register your marriage for protection? Set up some marital agreements or covenants. You and your spouse need to have the attitude of, "I'm stuck with you so let's figure this out!" Developing and having that attitude of you two against the world and not quitting is a mentality that you need to foster and develop in your marriage. No talk of if it doesn't get better, I'm leaving. No threatening divorce in an argument, even if you don't intend to actually get divorced. Threatening to leave may get your spouse's attention, but it also tells your spouse that the marriage is not as valuable as either of you may think. This is a habit that must be broken. Threatening to leave usually does more harm than good. Using talk like, "we need to figure this out," or, "how are we going to get along?" or, "what should we do?" all convey and send the message that you're not going anywhere, so we need to solve this. Make an agreement that no matter what happens in the course of your marriage, either one of you has the right to call for help, and you both will go together to get help. Hopefully this help comes in the form of a professional marriage counselor. Seeking out a pastor or a married couple that you respect can also be an option. Make this agreement clear and specific. Included in this book is a warranty card that you can print out to remember your agreement! Don't try to do this during a fight. Wait until you have resolved your argument and are in a good place.

The other big piece necessary for having some security in your marriage is making sure that God plays a significant part. When you're both working in tandem with God, it's no longer you two against the world but you, your spouse, and God! Those are much better odds. Most couples will choose to get married in a church or have a pastor marry them. That is an excellent way to start your marriage. The old saying goes, "Don't only invite Him to the wedding, keep Him in the marriage." Keep God in your marriage!

There are some powerful ways that you can do just that. Do devotionals together. Spend some time together reading and talking about God's plans for you and your marriage. Just finding the time sends the message that this is an important

 PRAYING TOGETHER IS SHARING WITH YOUR SPOUSE YOUR RELATIONSHIP WITH GOD

activity that needs to be done. Start slow, and don't make it too complicated. There are thousands of books and devotionals out there. Find one. Read it ... together. As you do this more, you will get more comfortable talking and sharing. Start first with just the questions included in the book, then over time, you can add your own questions. Don't get intimated or shy. Stay focused on the goal. How do you think you will feel if you get to hear your spouse's thoughts on God? If that sounds like a good thing, remember that you need to share yours as well.

Once you are doing devotionals, then you need to move towards praying together. Devotions are sharing your thoughts about God with your spouse. **Praying together is sharing your relationship with God with your spouse.** That is cool, but hard. Praying together will take some time. Some helpful hints are remembering that it's intimate to be able to hear your spouse talk to God. Be careful and make sure you treat those moments with respect. It would be best if you didn't make too many comments, critiques, or suggestions about how the prayer time went. Make praying together a safe place. Don't use prayer as a weapon on your spouse. The more intimate and personal the prayer is, the more benefits it has for your marriage. This kind of prayer is usually hard to do, so you probably won't be able to jump right into praying together. Start slow. You might start by praying at meals or reading prayers after your devotionals, and then you can gradually make them more personal. Take turns praying so that one spouse doesn't end up doing it all. This is an activity that you want to grow in and do together. Including a growing joint relationship with you, God, and your spouse will provide some protection when things begin to become challenging in your marriage.

Please take the time to fulfill the warranty on your marriage. At the end of this book is an image of a marriage warranty. If you go to **www.tonyboer.com** you will find a link where you can put your names in and print the warranty out.

WARRANTY INFORMATION

— NOTES —

CONCLUSION

This book/manual was written with the hope that you could take these tools and use them to make a healthy marriage for you and your spouse. Marriage is work. Hard work. But it is worth it. Having someone in your life that makes you feel loved, valuable, and like you matter is a fabulous feeling that can make your life feel amazing.

Feel free to email me feedback on how your relationship is going. I can be reached at www.tonyboer.com.

MARRIAGE WARRANTY

This marriage is under warranty. The parties involved have pledged to install, use, and repair all the tools to craft a healthy marriage. To keep warranty valid, they have pledged to provide the required routine maintenance for the lifetime of the marriage.

_____
Date

_____
Signatures

APPENDIX A

AREAS OF POTENTIAL CONFLICT

Here are some basic starter questions that you and your spouse should have talked about before you got married. If you didn't, don't worry, start now. You don't need to have complete agreement on these questions, but you should discuss them and have knowledge about your spouse's feelings on these issues. Come to some type of agreement or compromise. This is not an exhaustive list, but simply a place to start that will get the discussion going a little deeper.

—APPENDIX A—
AREAS OF POTENTIAL CONFLICT

1. **Work:** Should there be one or two wage-earners in the family?
   Is it okay to work part-time?
   How do you feel about working late or on weekends?
   How do you feel about travel for employment?
   How do family time and work time fit together?

2. **Income:** How much money do you need to be happy?
   What debt do you bring to this relationship?
   How much money do you need in your savings account to feel safe?
   How responsible would you say you are with money?
   Separate or joint accounts?
   Who will be managing the bills?
   Have you ever used or followed a budget?

3. **Housing:** House or apartment?
   Willing to relocate?
   Willing to live in the same town as your parents or in-laws?

4. **Children:** Do you want children?
   How many?
   How do you want your children to be cared for? Daycare? Stay-at-home?
   What is your parenting philosophy?
5. **Family:** What topics are off-limits to share with relatives?
   How much visiting and involvement with relatives do you like?
   How often do you talk with or visit your parents?
6. **Friends:** Which friendships are you wanting to keep after marriage? Which ones are you not?
   What is your attitude towards opposite-sex friendships? What are the expectations?
7. **Roles:** What are your expectations with housework? Childcare? Employment? Who is doing what?
8. **Activities:** How often do you want to go out separately? With friends? As a couple?
   What type of activities do you like to do? Cost? Time?
9. **Religion:** Do you share religious beliefs?
   How strong or important are your beliefs?
   How important is church attendance?

APPENDIX B

QUESTIONS USUALLY COVERED IN PREMARITAL COUNSELING SESSIONS

Here are some questions and topics that I usually cover in premarital counseling. Please remember that these are not a test to see if you are qualified to be together or get married, but they're typically topics or issues that will be talked about in marriage. Remember, the goal in premarital counseling is to learn who your spouse is, not to change them. Your spouse most likely won't change drastically over the course of your marriage. Understanding why your spouse acts a certain way provides you with an understanding of how to deal with them more effectively. Take your time and be thorough in answering these questions. I have the questions broken up by session.

—APPENDIX B—
QUESTIONS USUALLY COVERED IN PREMARITAL COUNSELING SESSIONS

SESSION 1: DATING HISTORY

Review your dating history. How did you meet? What did you like about each other? Any breakups while dating? Why? What made you finally decide to get married? What made you ask her? Were you surprised when he asked, or had you talked about it and simply didn't know when he was asking but knew you would be getting married? How did others respond to the news? Parents? Friends? Take a little time and describe your future spouse. How would you define him or her?

SESSION 2: FAMILY HISTORY

Are your parents still married? Divorced? Reasons for divorce? Would you want the same marriage your parents had? Why or why not? Did you have good role models of what you should be or act like in a marriage? Do you know what you expect of a wife or husband?

SESSION 3: PERSONALITY

Who are you, really? Does your spouse know? How do you act when you are mad? Do you show your feelings easily or keep them hidden? Yell or quiet? Do you know how to fight healthy and fair? Do you know the difference between giving in and compromising? What do you need when you're scared? Angry? Lonely?

SESSION 4: MONEY

Who will pay the bills? What are your financial goals? How much money can you spend without asking? Are you going to have a budget? Are you a penny pincher or a spender? What debt are you bringing into the marriage? How are you going to handle things if one of you makes more money than the other? Joint or separate accounts?

SESSION 5: SEX

Where did you learn about sex? Is your spouse aware of your dating history? What are your expectations of sex in marriage? How are you going to handle it when you and your spouse have different drives? How much have you communicated about children, and how many would you like to have? Do you want to be married a while or have children right away?

SESSION 6: RELIGION

What religious background did you grow up in? How often did you attend church? What do you need or want in a church? How do you want your children raised? What are the traditions in your church, and what is the theology of

Questions usually covered in Premarital Counseling Sessions

your church? Are you willing to change religions? Churches? What are your expectations of your spouse? Why is grace so important in marriage?

APPENDIX C

HOW TO GET YOUR SPOUSE TO GO TO MARRIAGE COUNSELING

If you want to go to marriage counseling and your spouse is reluctant, here are some things you can try to achieve that goal. In general, couples wait too long before they actually go to counseling. Unfortunately, most couples go in a last-ditch effort to try and save a sinking ship instead of coming in for a tune-up to keep the marriage on the right track.

— APPENDIX C —

HOW TO GET YOUR SPOUSE TO GO TO MARRIAGE COUNSELING

1. Don't bring up going to marriage counseling when you're in the middle of a fight. The last thing your spouse wants is to do "this" (i.e., fight) in front of someone else. Too often the only time marriage counseling is brought up is when things are in crisis mode. When things settle down, couples tend to not talk about counseling. This associates marriage counseling with arguments or a forum for how I'm going to tell you how bad you are.

2. Convey to your spouse why you want to go to counseling. Can you articulate where you're getting stuck and where you're having trouble? If you can't identify a reason why you need to go to counseling, you have the wrong frame of mind. Saying things like, "I would like to go to counseling to better understand how to connect with you," sends a better message than, "We need to go to counseling because you are such a jerk, and I can't stand to be around you unless you change!" I know that sounds a little exaggerated, but I can assure you that it is more accurate than you may believe.

3. Can you convey how important it is to you that you go to counseling? Is it a suggestion or an ultimatum? Where are you at with your feelings on how the marriage is going? Sometimes it helps to use a number scale. How bad is your marriage?

1 2 3 4 5 6 7 8 9 10

Fairytale/Never leaving   Not great but not terrible   Bags are packed/Leaving

Each of you can put down a number and then share. Your numbers most likely are not the same. That's okay, but you're trying to convey that you simply want to learn how to get your number lower.

4. The focus of marriage counseling is to learn and grow, not to prove who is right and who is wrong.

5. Are you willing to go to counseling by yourself if your spouse doesn't go? You will need to convey that to your spouse. Follow through, if it isn't that important to you that you're not willing to go alone, then you're sending that message to your spouse.

6. Ask your spouse what their "line in the sand" is of when they think marriage counseling would be necessary or when they would be willing to go.

7. Does either of you know any couples who have gone to counseling? What were that couple's impressions? Do they have any suggestions for you?

ABOUT THE AUTHOR

Tony Boer is a therapist in Sioux Falls, SD. He founded Sioux Empire Christian counseling to help individuals and families learn how to deal with challenges, grow, and thrive. Tony has spoken and presented on a variety of topics, including marriage, adoption, and autism. In addition, Tony provides supervision and consultation to fellow therapists. He has also written a book called *The Art of Therapy,* to guide other therapists in using his unique brand of insights and interventions. Tony has been married to Michelle since 1993. They have three children, Michaela, Anna, and Jacob.

REFERENCES/RESOURCES

i. Boer, Tony. *The Art of Therapy: A Practical How-To Guide for Therapists.* Story Seven Publishing, 2020.

ii. Wheat, Ed. *The First Years of Forever.* Grand Rapids, Michigan, Zondervan, 1988.

iii. Chapman, Gary. *The Five Love Languages: How to Express Heartfelt Commitment to your Mate.* Northfield Publishing, 2004.

iv. VanLaningam J, Johnson DR, Amato Pr. "Marital Happiness, Marital Duration, and the U-Shaped Curve: Evidence from a Five-Wave Panel Study," Social Forces, 2001: 79:1313-1341.

v. Aaron A, Norman C, Aaron E, Lewandowski G. "Shared Participation in Self-Expanding Activities," Understanding Marriage: Developments in the Study of Couple Interaction. New York: Cambridge University Press; 2002. Pp. 177-194.

vi. Gray, John. *Men are from Mars, Women are from Venus: A Practical Guide for Improving Communication and Getting What you want in your Relationships.* New York, Harper Collins, 1992.

vii. Farrell, Bill, Farrell Pam. *Men are like Waffles—Women are like Spaghetti.* Eugene Oregon, Harvest House, 2001.

www.ingramcontent.com/pod-product-compliance
Lightning Source LLC
Chambersburg PA
CBHW071233070526
44583CB00017B/2165